Praise for APA Made Easy

"This book delivers. What a splendid, visual quick start guide to APA formatting! Readers will benefit not only from the author's candid and concise advice on APA, but also from his sometimes witty and entertaining style. Thanks for making this such a quick, straightforward, and fun read!" - *Dr. Todd D. Vasquez*

I bought the book for my kindle. This book is very clear and concise. I needed it in a hurry too. The book gives you step by step instructions, with illustrations, on how to set up your document. It's "idiot proof". Then to make it more "idiot proof" inside the book is a link to the books' webpage where you can download a template for Windows Office and Apple Pages. I would buy this book again and recommend it my friends, my Mom, a stranger, the Pope or anyone who needs to write in APA. - *Shelly Stewart Amazon.com 5 star review*

I have already been using this book and to me it is a great tool for those students who need to use the APA format. I am so happy that I got this little book for my own personal reference guide. I am an adult student and this book will be a life saver for me. It is small enough that I am able to put it into my folder and take to my classes. I always have it handy when I need it for my own reference. This is my first time using the APA format and this little book has a gold mine of information for us students needing to learn the format for our papers in school. Do I recommend this book? Absolutely! - *Theresa Wolfe, Amazon 5 Star Review*

This book is so great that it makes me want to cry! I am using it right now to finish my master's thesis and it is exactly what I needed. I really wish I had been able to use this from the start of my degrees. It is just the perfect way to introduce a student to formatting and citations according to a particular style. - *Amazon.com 5 Star Review*

This book was written perfectly. It guided me step by step in formatting my paper in clear easy to understand way. Very straightforward. Would definitely recommend it! - *Amazon 5 Star Review*

THE BIG BOOK OF APA CITATIONS AND REFERENCES

"Complete, thorough, and simply indispensable for any college student"

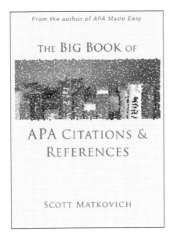
The Big Book of APA Citations and References is the definitive guide to getting every reference right. In response to dozens of web sites and online APA reference generators that often lead students down the wrong path, each reference has been meticulously checked against the Sixth Edition of the APA Manual for Publication for accuracy. Included in this book are references for:

• Books • Journals • Magazines • Newspapers • Media • Reviews
• Social Media • Online Posts • Newsletters • Unpublished Manuscripts
• Peer Commentary • Collections • Legal Documents • Research Reports
• Data Sets and Much More!

AVAILABLE NOW ON AMAZON.COM

All information in this book is in accordance with the 6th Edition of the APA Manual.

To view or print any of the charts in this book visit:

www.YouVersusTheWorld.com

Table of Contents

Chapter from Book with Editor Only
Social Media: Facebook and Twitter
Online Book Review

Preface to the Third Edition - Paperback Edition

To say that I am overwhelmed and grateful for the support of this book is an understatement. For all of you who bought the previous editions of this book, I am sending a huge "Thank you!" a hundred times over!! This third edition is for you.

New to this version are: instructions for creating an APA formatted paper in Microsoft Word 2013 and Word 2011 for Mac, an expanded reference and citation guide, and more detail and background information around formatting references. All of the charts in this book are available to you on my website: www.YouVersusTheWorld.com (see the So Now What? Read This First section for the password!).

I realize that this book is packed with information around APA formatting. Because I know its hard to find bits of information as needed, I decided to structure the book in the same "flow" as an APA formatted paper. The general flow of this book is as follows:

Title pages and abstracts > Writing the Body of Your Paper > Headings > In Text Citations > References > Tables, Figures and Appendices > Other Writing Advice.

Additionally, using the search feature on your tablet or computer will produce an index of any term in this book, which can be very helpful.

My goal with this book has never been to simply "deliver the goods". *I am in this with you.* If you use this book and find that it doesn't answer a formatting or stylistic question that you need for your paper, simply send me an email with your question to scott@apamadeeasy.com, and I will do my best to get you back on track.

You guys are amazing. Thanks again for your support!

Scott Matkovich
Dacono, CO
June 20th, 2013

Introduction

First, thank you for your interest in APA Made Easy. Let me take a minute to discuss why I would write a step-by-step guide to APA formatting. After all, how boring does one need to be to write something like this? While I may be accused of being boring (just don't ask my wife), after teaching for a number of years both in the classroom and online, one consistent "thorn in the flesh" of my students has been APA formatting. By writing a step-by-step guide I hope to:

a) Help take the confusion out of the writing process and surrounding the APA in general.

b) Provide an immediate starting point for those unfamiliar with APA.

Having been a student before, I know the feeling of being tired at the end of the day, having to write a paper before bed, opening the word processor just to sit and stare blankly at the screen for 5 minutes not knowing where to start. If you use these guides for Word 2010, Word 2013, Pages, or Word 2011 for Mac, you will never have to stare at the screen again!

Along with an APA walkthrough for both Mac and PC users, I also provide a sample outline of a paper, and talk about how to structure a research paper for greater clarity. Also included are "quick guides" that you can refer to without having to reread entire sections. If you follow these steps, you will notice an increase in your motivation to write and communicate well. Remember, writing is an art form that needs to be practiced. While there is a right and wrong way to format a paper, APA format should serve only as a canvas for your artwork to be displayed!

One final note: my intention was not to create a comprehensive APA guide. My focus was on helping students get the majority (I would guess 90%) of what they need fast. I realize that there are components missing, and there are great (much longer and more detailed) books, websites and resources for those who are more exacting.

Happy writing!

Scott Matkovich

How to Use This Guide

With the goal of helping both Mac and PC users, I have designed this guide with two separate (but not necessarily distinct) sections. The first section is designed as a walkthrough for setting up any paper in APA format. The second section works more around formatting after you start writing. Whenever possible, I include screenshots to help easily locate the appropriate menus on your computer. Also, I decided to italicize any menu paths such as:

Home (in the menu bar) > Styles > Click Change Styles > Style Set > Manuscript Style.

You will notice that I also try to add helpful notes in with the menu paths. While it may not be very formal, I don't consider myself to be too formal either - so there it is! Also, take my suggestions for writing a paper for what they are: *suggestions.* My highest hope for you is to develop your own style and method. And, if you already have one, don't feel obligated to use mine if you think yours is better.

Comments? Questions? Concerns? I would love to hear from you! I can be reached directly at scott@apamadeeasy.com.

Creating an APA Document in Microsoft Word 2010

Before you begin, please note that there are completed templates for Microsoft Word 2010 available on my website. To find them, click "Templates" in the menu bar and choose which format you would like to download. This is a good option for those who are in a hurry get writing.

Open Microsoft Word by selecting it from Start > All Programs > Microsoft Office > Microsoft Word 2010.

Page 1 - The Title Page

Before you begin you will want to change the settings now as they will remain the same throughout the rest of the document.

First, let's change our font to Times New Roman size 12. This is the recommendation of the APA.

- Click *Home > Font > Times New Roman*. The box just to the right of Times New Roman, *click the selection arrow and select 12*.

Second, make sure that the borders of your document are all 1 inch. The APA requires a 1 inch border for all documents.

- We can check the borders by clicking *Page Layout in the menu > click Margins > Normal.*

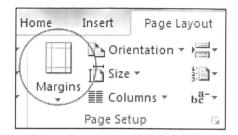

- We will want our entire document to be double spaced. We can double space our document though Quick Style by clicking *Home (in the menu bar) > Styles > Click Change Styles > Style Set > Manuscript Style.*

The Manuscript style is set to double space the entire document.

- Another way to achieve the same result is to click *Home > Paragraph (expand the box) > Spacing > Double.*

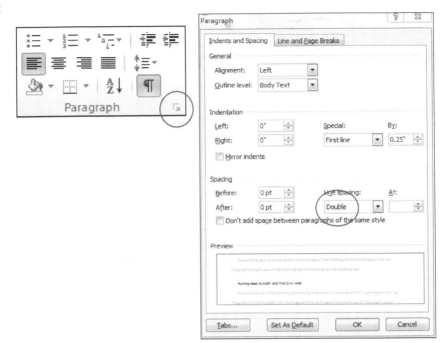

- The APA rules require a running head and short title for every paper. However, before we enter the header for the title page, we need to go to: Insert *(on menu bar)* > Header > Edit Header *(toward the bottom of the menu)*. At this point you should notice a green Header Design box in the upper right corner of the document. In the *Design Tab > Options > select Different First Page.*

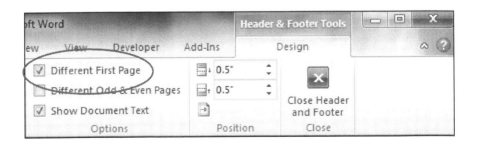

Type: "Running head: SHORT TITLE OF YOUR PAPER".

What is a short title? The short title of your paper is the title in 50 characters or less. However, your Short title should still make sense to the reader. That may mean that you need to shorten the title of your paper by offering a condensed version of the title. For example:

THE META-ETHICAL PROBLEM OF EVIL IN THE WRITINGS OF CALVIN

can be condensed to:

THE PROBLEM OF EVIL IN THE WRITINGS OF CALVIN

The term "Running head:" should *only appear on our title page.* After that, the short title of our paper should be the only text in the header.

Running head: SLAVERY AND THE CIVIL WAR¶

First Page Header

- Next, we need to insert page numbers. While still in the Header Design (green) tab, move your cursor to the end of your header title. Find the Position section and click the *Insert Alignment Tab > select Right Alignment.*

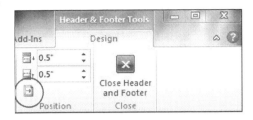

- Your cursor should be blinking on the top right margin of your page. Now, click *Page Number in the Header and Footer section > Current Position > Plain Number*.

The header for your title page is now complete. Click the *Close Header and Footer button*. Your cursor should jump back to the left margin of your paper.

Now we are ready to fill in our title, your name, and the name of the university or institution we are writing for. By now, your paper should be formatted to automatically double space every time we press Enter/Return.

- *Press Return/Enter (5) times and Center your cursor by Clicking Home > Paragraph section > Center Text (or Ctrl + E).*

- Type the title of your paper. Be sure to capitalize all essential words.

- Press *Return/Enter* once and type your name. Do not include any titles with your name (Dr., Mr., Ph.D, etc.).

- Press *Enter* once and type the name of the university or institution you are writing for.

Once you have entered the university or institution name, press *Return/Enter* once. Because we have everything required by the APA on our title page, we can insert a page break.

- Click *Page Layout (in menu bar) > in Page Setup section click Breaks > Page. Your cursor will jump to the second page.* Adding a Page Break will ensure that no other writing accidentally spills onto your title page.

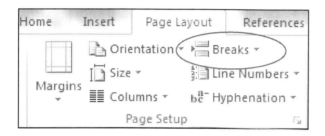

By now, your title page should look like this:

16

Running head: SLAVERY AND THE CIVIL WAR → 1¶

¶

¶

¶

¶

¶

Slavery and the Civil War¶

Bill R. Johnson¶

University of Sydney¶

----------------Page Break----------------¶

Tips for your Title page:

What we have completed so far fulfills the APA's requirements for a title page. However, if you feel you should add other elements such as the date, instructor name, or other information, check with your instructor first.

Additionally, the APA manual recommends using Times New Roman as the font for your paper. If you desire to use another font, be sure to get your instructors permission before doing so.

Page 2: Abstract

Abstracts are rarely required for college papers. In fact, if you include one without checking first with your instructor you run the risk of falling under the required word count of the paper should the instructor not count the abstract. However, if you are required to include one, we will walk through it step by step!

Formatting First!

By now, you have already completed 90% of the formatting you will need for your entire paper. However, there is one thing we need to fix before moving on. We need to reenter the title of our paper on the second page header, this time *without* the words, "Running head:"

Your cursor should still be oriented to the center of the paper, but if not go to the menu bar and click *Center Page*.

• **Type** "Abstract".

After we have established the Abstract page, we can simply repeat our steps to set our header and page numbers.

Insert > Header > Blank.

At this point, the cursor may jump back to the title page. If so, simply scroll back down to the Abstract page. Also, your font may have shifted back to a default size and font. This can be changed by going to the Home tab and clicking Times New Roman and 12 for size.

• Type your SHORT TITLE in all caps. Remember, this time we leave "Running head:" out of the header.

Now to enter our page number again.

• *Insert > Header and Footer Tools Design Tab > Position section > Insert Alignment Tab > Right > Page Number (Header and Footer section) > Current Position > Plain Number.*

The number "2" should appear on your page. Close the Header and Footer Design tab, and your cursor will reappear after the word "Abstract".

SLAVERY AND THE CIVIL WAR → 2¶

Header

Abstract¶

- Press *Enter* once, align your cursor to the left (Ctrl+L), and begin typing your abstract <u>without</u> an indentation. Your page should look similar to this:

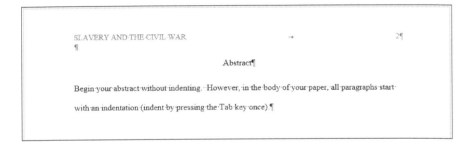

SLAVERY AND THE CIVIL WAR → 2¶
¶
Abstract¶

Begin your abstract without indenting. However, in the body of your paper, all paragraphs start with an indentation (indent by pressing the Tab key once).¶

- Click *Page Layout (in menu bar) > in Page Setup section click Breaks > Page. Your cursor will jump to the third page.*

Page 3 - The Main Body

All the formatting that you need is now in place, and you can begin writing your paper. After the walkthrough section of this book, you will find topics that continue to guide your writing in the body of your paper including: organizing your writing, headings, in text citations, and the dreaded reference page! Of course, feel free to navigate other resources in this book as you need them.

Creating an APA Document in Microsoft Word 2013

Before you begin, please note that there are completed templates for Microsoft Word 2010 available on my website. To find them, click "Templates" in the menu bar and choose which format you would like to download. This is a good option for those who are in a hurry get writing.

- Open Microsoft Word by selecting it from Start > All programs > Microsoft Office > Microsoft Word 2013. Choose "Blank Document".

Page 1 – The Title Page

Before you begin you will want to change the settings now as they will remain the same throughout the rest of the document.

- First, let's change our font to Times New Roman size 12. This is the recommendation of the APA.

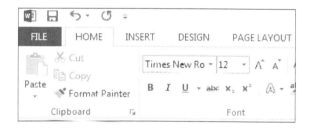

- Click Home > locate the font drop down box > select Times New Roman. Alternatively, press Ctrl + Shift + F. Locate the font box and select Times New Roman.

Second, make sure that the borders of your document are all 1 inch. The APA requires a 1 inch border for all documents.

- We can check the borders by clicking Page Layout (in the menu bar) > Margins > Normal.

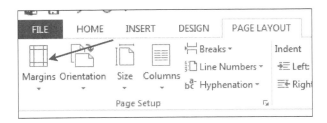

- Based on APA standards, our entire document should be double spaced. We can double space our document by clicking Home > Line and Paragraph Spacing tab > select 2.0.

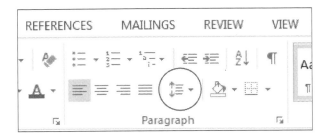

Next we will set our header and short title for our paper. The APA requires that every paper have a short title in the header position. A short title is the title of your paper in 50 characters or less. Most often, this simply means you will leave out any subtitles in your header.

- To set the header for your title page, click Insert > Header > Blank.

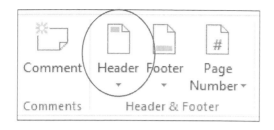

- After selecting your Blank header, you should see a green "Header and Footer Tools" box appear in the Design Tab. Before typing your Running head, check the box labeled "Different First Page".

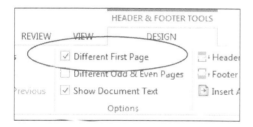

Now we are ready to type the Running head. Type the words "Running head: SHORT TITLE OF YOUR PAPER.

What is a short title? The short title of your paper is the title in 50 characters or less. However, your Short title should still make sense to the reader. That may mean that you need to shorten the title of your paper by offering a condensed version of the title. For example:

THE META-ETHICAL PROBLEM OF EVIL IN THE WRITINGS OF CALVIN

can be condensed to:

THE PROBLEM OF EVIL IN THE WRITINGS OF CALVIN

The term "Running head:" should only appear on our title page. After that, the short title of our paper should be the only text in the header.

Double check to make sure Word has kept your header font in Times New Roman. Microsoft Word has a bad habit of forgetting the formatting when it comes to headers and footers! If you need to change the font, simply highlight the entire header text with your mouse. You will see a formatting box appear where you can change the font and font size.

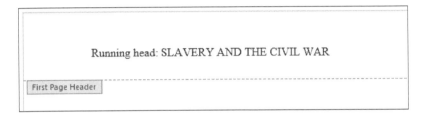

After we have typed our Running head, we can insert our page numbers. If we just try to insert a page number, our Running head will disappear! Because of this glitch in Word, we have to manually enter our page number.

- Here's how: With our cursor immediately after our short title, find the Position section and click Insert Alignment Tab > select Right Alignment. Click "OK".

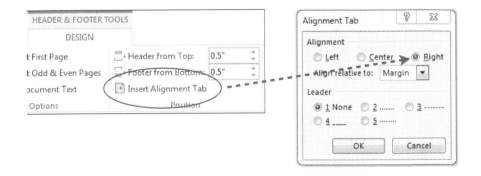

- Your cursor should be blinking on the top right margin of your page. Now, select the Page Number icon > Current Position > Plain Number.

- Double click underneath the First Page Header dotted line to deselect the header or simply click the "Close Header and Footer" icon. The header and page number will both turn light gray.

The completed header should now look like this:

We are now ready to finish the rest of our title page by filling in our full title, name, and the name of the university or institution we are writing for. By now, your paper should be formatted to automatically double space each time we press Enter/Return.

- Press Enter (5) times and Center your cursor by clicking Home > locating the Paragraph section > select Center Text (or Ctrl + E).

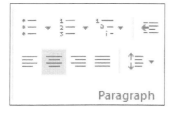

First, type the full title of your paper. Be sure to capitalize all essential words. Press Enter once and type your name. Do not include any titles with your name (Dr., Mr., Ph.D, etc.).

Once you have entered the university or institution name, press enter once. Because we have everything required by the APA on our title page, we can insert a page break. This will keep any other writing from spilling onto our title page.

• Click Page Layout (in the menu bar) > in the Page Setup section click Breaks > Page. Your cursor will jump to the second page.

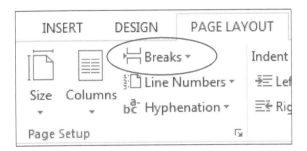

By now your title page should look like this:

Running head: SLAVERY AND THE CIVIL WAR   →   1¶

¶

¶

¶

¶

Slavery and the Civil War¶

Bill R. Johnson¶

University of Sydney¶

·····Page Break·····¶

Page 2: Abstract

Abstracts are rarely required for undergraduate college papers. In fact, if you include one without checking first with your instructor, you may run the risk of falling under the required word count of the paper should the instructor not count the words in the abstract. However, if you are required to include an abstract, we will walk through it step by step!

Formatting First!

By now, you have already completed 90% of the formatting you will need for your entire paper! However, there is one thing we need to fix before moving on.

- At this point, your cursor should still be oriented to the center of the paper, but if not click (Ctrl + E) or click Home > locate the Paragraph section > click Center.

- Type "Abstract".

After we have established the Abstract page, we can simply repeat our steps to set our header and page numbers.

- Click Insert (on the menu) > click Header > Blank.

At this point, the cursor may jump back to the title page. If so, simply scroll back down to the Abstract page.

- Type your SHORT TITLE in all caps. Remember, this time we are leaving "Running head:" out of the header.

Again, the font of your header may have shifted back to the default font and size. You can change the font by highlighting the text and selecting Times New Roman and 12 for the font size from the pop-up box.

- Now to enter our page numbers again. Click Insert > click Header and Footer Tools Design (the green tab) > locate the Position section > click Insert Alignment tab > Right. Click "OK".

- Your cursor will move all the way to the right corner of your paper. Next click Insert > the Page Number icon > Current Position > Plain number. The number 2 should appear on the page. Close the Header and Footer Design tab and your cursor will reappear with the word "Abstract".

Position your cursor immediately after the word "Abstract".

- Press Enter once, align your cursor to the left (Ctrl + L), and begin typing your abstract without an indentation. Your page should look similar to this:

SLAVERY AND THE CIVIL WAR   28

Abstract

Begin your abstract without indenting. However, in the body of your paper, all paragraphs start

with an indentation (indent by pressing the Tab key once).

After you finish typing your abstract, press Return/Enter once and insert a page break. This will keep the body of your paper from spilling back onto the abstract page. Here's how:

• Click Insert (from the menu bar) > click Page Break icon.

All the formatting that you need is now in place, and you can begin writing your paper. After the walkthrough section of this book, you will find topics that continue to guide your writing in the body of your paper including: organizing your writing, headings, in text citations, and the dreaded reference page! Of course, feel free to navigate other resources in this book as you need them.

Creating an APA Document for Apple Pages

Before you begin, please note that there are completed templates for Microsoft Word 2010 available on my website. To find them, click "Templates" in the menu bar and choose which format you would like to download. This is a good option for those who are in a hurry get writing.

Open Pages by selecting it from the Applications folder.

Page 1 - The Title Page

Before you begin you will want to change the settings now as they will remain the same throughout the rest of the document.

- Open the Inspector: *View > Show Inspector.* For sake of ease, you may just want to add the Inspector to your toolbar items (It shows up by default, unless you have removed it previously). *Hold the Control button and Click > Customize Toolbar > Drag the Inspector Tab to the toolbar.*

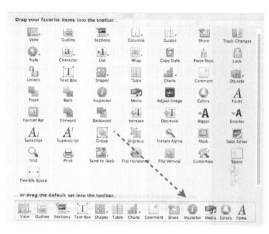

Within the Inspector window, there are several different inspectors that you will need to know as I will refer to them later on. Notice that the name of each inspector shows up at the top of the Inspector box. In order from left to right:

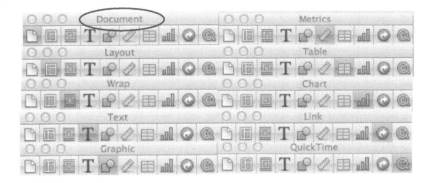

- In the Inspector window select the *Document Inspector.* In the Spacing section, check to make sure your margins are all set to 1 inch. All APA documents have 1 inch margins on all sides.

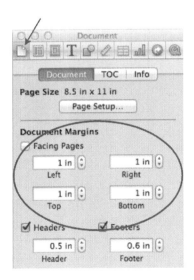

- In the Inspector window, select *Text Inspector*. In the Spacing section, locate where the Line Spacing is, and *change it from Single to Double.* You can also move the slider until the Line Spacing shows a "2".

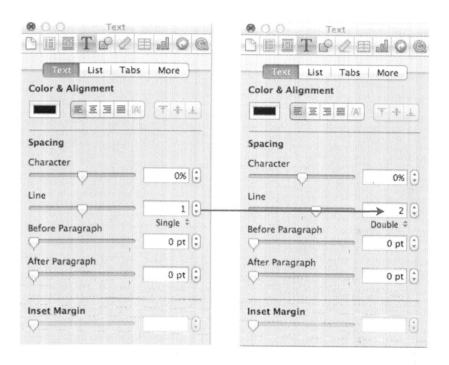

Close the Inspector window for now.

- Click *View* in the toolbar and choose *Show Layout.* You can see the header and footer areas at the top and bottom of the page. Select the header at the top of the page and make sure your cursor is all the way to the left of the header box. You can also view the header by rolling over it with your mouse. (If it is in the center or the right of the box:

- *View > Show Inspector > Text Inspector > Under Color and Alignment, click Align Text to the Left*).

- Before typing the header, we need to do one more thing to save some time in the future. Open the Inspector and select the Layout Inspector. *Under the Section > Configuration section, click First page is different.*

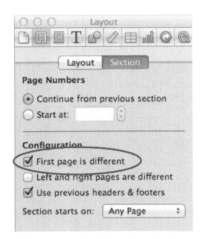

- Now you are ready to enter your Running head. Type "Running head: SHORT TITLE OF YOUR PAPER.

What is a short title? The short title of your paper is the title in 50 characters or less. However, your Short title should still make sense to the reader. That may mean that you need to shorten the title of your paper by offering a condensed version of the title. For example:

THE META-ETHICAL PROBLEM OF EVIL IN THE WRITINGS OF CALVIN

can be condensed to:

THE PROBLEM OF EVIL IN THE WRITINGS OF CALVIN

Your Running head short title should be no longer then 50 words and in all CAPS. Note: the words "Running head:" should only appear on your title page. Thereafter, the short title of your page should just appear in the header. Our sample paper will be on Slavery and the Civil War. Here is how it should appear on the Title page.

> Running head: SLAVERY AND THE CIVIL WAR

• Now we insert our page numbers.

In the menu bar, click *Insert > Auto Page Number.* A menu box will pop up. The options should read:

- Show in: **Document**
- **Check box** for "Include number on first page."
- Position: **Header**
- Alignment: **Right**
- Format: 1,2,3
- Click *Insert*.

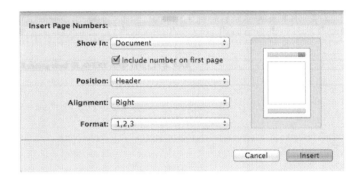

The number 1 should appear on your title page, the number 2 on the second page and so forth.

- Press the Return key **5** times. Each time you press the key, the cursor should automatically double space. (If not, repeat step 2).

- Click *View > Show Inspector > Text Inspector > locate the Color & Alignment section and click Center Text*. You will notice your cursor jump to the center of the page.

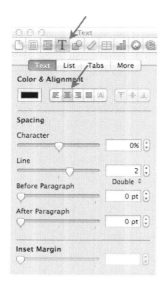

- Type in the Title of your paper. Make sure you capitalize any essential words (any words other than and, of, it/its, the, etc.) and click Return once.

- Type your first, middle initial, last name. Do not use title or degrees such as (Dr. or Ph.D) in your name. Press Return *once*.

- Type in the name of the university or college you are doing research for and press Return *once*.

36

```
┌─────────────────────────────────────────────────────────────┐
│ Running head: SLAVERY AND THE CIVIL WAR                     1 │
└─────────────────────────────────────────────────────────────┘

┌─────────────────────────────────────────────────────────────┐
│                                                               │
│                                                               │
│                                                               │
│                                                               │
│                    Slavery and the Civil War                  │
│                         Bill R. Johnson                       │
│                      University of Sydney                     │
│                                                               │
│                                                               │
└─────────────────────────────────────────────────────────────┘
```

- Finally, on the menu bar select *Insert > Page Break*. Page break will automatically take you to the second page of your document. You have successfully created a proper APA title page! Great job! Your completed title page should look like this:

You can now save this title page as a Template for future papers! File > Save as Template. I recommend that you name the file "My APA Template."

- When you are ready to retrieve your template click *File > New from Template Chooser > In the Left Column click My Templates > My APA Template. Click Save.*

Tips for your Title page:

What we have completed so far fulfills the APA's requirements for a title page. However, if you feel you should add other elements such as the date, instructor name, or other information, check with your instructor first.

The APA manual recommends using Times New Roman as the font for your paper. If you desire to use another font, be sure to get your instructors permission before doing so.

Page 2 - The Abstract

Abstracts are rarely required for college papers. In fact, if you include one without checking first with your instructor you run the risk of falling under the required word count of the paper should the instructor not count the abstract. However, if you are required to include one, we will walk through it step by step!

Formatting First!

By now, you have already completed 90% of the formatting you will need for your entire paper. However, there is one thing we need to fix before moving on. We need to reenter the title of our paper (in all CAPS) on the second page header, this time without the words, "Running head:"

Your cursor should still be oriented to the center of the paper, but if not go to the Text Inspector and *click Center Text.*

• Type "Abstract" and press Return once.

Then, go to the Text Inspector under Color and Alignment and click "Align text to the left." Now you can begin typing your abstract. Just remember, with abstracts you do not indent the first sentence of your paragraph as with the other paragraphs in your paper.

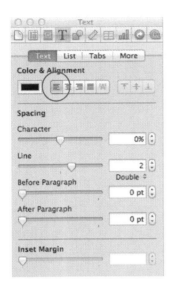

Your abstract is a summary of your work including the kind of research you have done, the results, and statistics and findings which are a part of your research and so forth. Your abstract should be concise and brief - between 200 - 250 words total.

- Once you are done with your abstract, press the Return key once, then click *Insert > Page Break*. This will start a new page where you can begin your paper.

All the formatting that you need is now in place, and you can begin writing your paper. After the walkthrough section of this book, you will find topics that continue to guide your writing in the body of your paper including: organizing your writing, headings, in text citations, and the dreaded reference page! Of course, feel free to navigate other resources in this book as you need them.

Creating an APA Document for Microsoft Word 2011 for Mac

Before you begin, please note that there are completed templates for Microsoft Word 2010 available on my website. To find them, click "Templates" in the menu bar and choose which format you would like to download. This is a good option for those who are in a hurry get writing.

Open Microsoft Word 2011 by pressing Command + Spacebar (Spotlight). Type Microsoft Word, and select it from the drop down menu.

Page 1 - The Title Page

Select "Word Document" from the Template menu.

First, let's change our font to Times New Roman size 12. This is the recommendation of the APA.

Click *Home > locate the Font section > Times New Roman.* The box just to the right of Times New Roman, *click the selection arrow and select 12.*

Second, the APA requires a 1 inch border for all documents. We can check the borders by clicking the *click Layout tab > locate the Margins section > click Margins icon > select Normal.* You may also manually set the margins to 1" using the Margins section if you prefer.

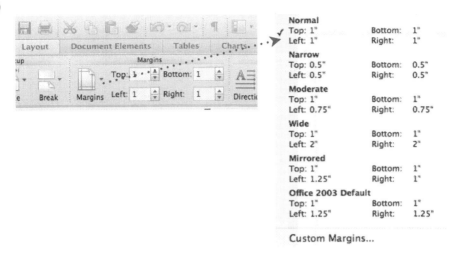

We will want our entire document to be double spaced. We can double space our document though Quick Style by clicking:

- *Format (in the menu bar) > Paragraph > Line Spacing > Double.*

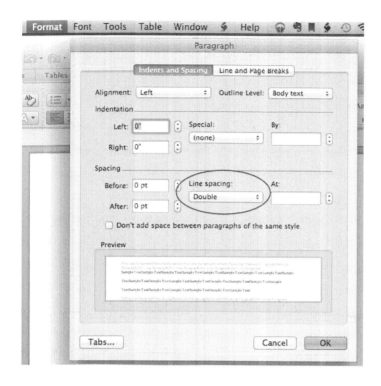

Another way to double space your paper is by clicking the Line Spacing icon in the Home Menu.

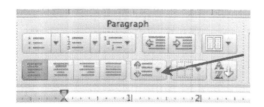

- *Select 2.0.*

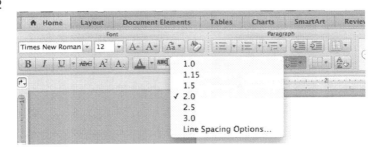

The APA rules require a running head and short title for our paper. However, before we enter the header for the title page, we need to go to:

• *Document Elements > Header > Basic (All Pages).*

You will notice that once you click the header button, a purple "Header and Footer" tab will appear. We will need this for the next step.

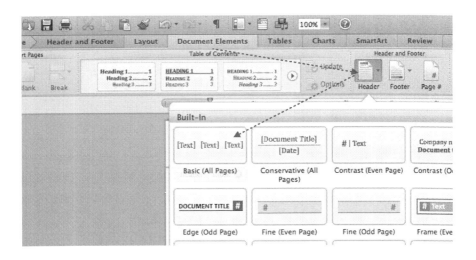

Before typing our running head, we need to select the purple *Header and Footer tab > Options > Different First Page.*

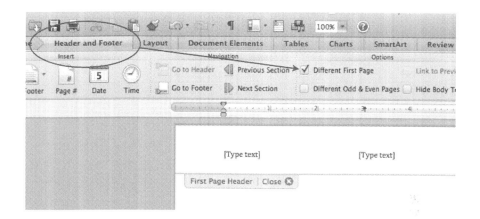

You will see the cursor blinking in the upper left hand corner of your paper.

Type: "Running head: SHORT TITLE OF YOUR PAPER".

What is a short title? The short title of your paper is the title in 50 characters or less. However, the Short title should still make sense to the reader. That may mean that we need to shorten the title of your paper by offering a condensed version of the title. For example:

THE META-ETHICAL PROBLEM OF EVIL IN THE WRITINGS OF CALVIN

can be condensed to:

THE PROBLEM OF EVIL IN THE WRITINGS OF CALVIN

According to the APA Manual, the term "Running head:" should *only appear on our title page.* After that, the short title of our paper should be the only text in the header.

- Be sure to follow the next few steps closely as Microsoft Word 2011 is notoriously tricky when entering the header text!

Next, we need to insert page numbers. In APA format, the title page gets a page number in the upper right-hand corner. With the cursor still placed after the header text, locate the *Insert section > click Page #.*

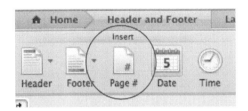

The page number will appear immediately after your running head.

Use your cursor to highlight the *page number only.* Click *Document Elements > locate the Header and Footer section > click Page #.* When the Page # pop-up comes up, select "Right" under Alignment, then click "Ok". The page number will move to the right.

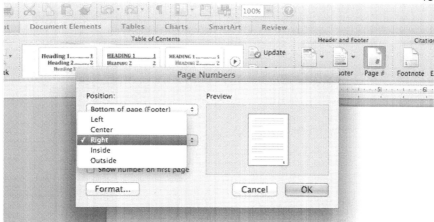

Close the Header and Footer section by clicking *Close*. The header and page number will turn light gray.

Your paper should now look like this:

Running head: SLAVERY AND THE CIVIL WAR   1

The header for your title page is now complete. Your cursor should now be back to the left margin of your paper.

We are ready to fill in our title, your name, and the name of the university or institution we are writing for. By now, your paper should be formatted to automatically double space every time we press Enter/Return.

Press Enter (5) times and Center your cursor by Clicking Home > locate the Paragraph section > click Center Text.

- Type the title of your paper. Be sure to capitalize all essential words.

- Press *Enter* once and type your name. Do not include any titles with your name (Dr., Mr., Ph.D, etc.).

- Press *Enter* once and type the name of the university or institution you are writing for.

Once you have entered the university or institution name, press *enter* once. Because we have everything required by the APA on our title page, we can insert a page break. This will keep other text from accidentally spilling onto this page.

- Click *Insert (in the menu bar) > Break > Page Break. Your cursor will jump to the second page.*

Your completed title page will look like this:

Slavery and the Civil War

Bill R. Johnson

University of Sydney

Tips for your Title page:

What we have completed so far fulfills the APA's requirements for a title page. However, if you feel you should add other elements such as the date, instructor name, or other information, check with your instructor first.

The APA manual recommends using Times New Roman as the font for your paper. If you desire to use another font, be sure to get your instructors permission before doing so.

Page 2: Abstract

Abstracts are rarely required for undergraduate college papers. In fact, if you include one without checking first with your instructor you run the risk of falling under the required word count of the paper should the instructor not count the abstract. However, if you are required to include one, we will walk through it step by step!

Formatting First!

Your cursor should still be oriented to the center of the paper, but if not go to the Text Inspector and click *Center Page.*

• **Type** "Abstract".

After we have established the Abstract page, we can simply re-enter our header and page numbers for the remainder of the paper. At this point the top of page two will probably be displaying a basic header:

[Type text]	[Type text]	[Type text]
	Abstract	

Hover your cursor over the header and you will see it turn into the header icon. Once you see this happen, *double click* and the header tab is now ready to edit with the cursor to the left of the first [Type Text] box.

Highlight and delete all three of the [Type Text] boxes.

• Type your SHORT TITLE in all caps. Remember, this time we leave "Running head:" out of the header.

Now to enter our page number again. Click *Document Elements > locate the Header and Foote*r section > *click Page #.* Under Alignment, select *Right.* Leave the "Show number on the first page" box unchecked.

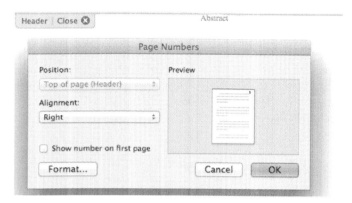

The number "2" should show up on your page. Close the Header and Footer Design tab, and your cursor will reappear after the word "Abstract".

Press *Enter* once, align your cursor to the left (Click *Home > locate the Paragraph section > click Align Text Left*), and begin typing your abstract without an indentation. Your page should look similar to this:

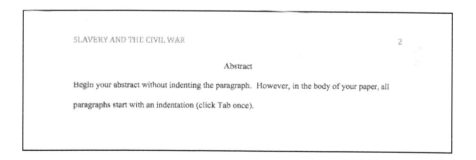

Once you have completed your abstract, press *enter* once, then create a page break by selecting:

• *Insert > Break > Page Break.*

Check to make sure your header and page numbers carry onto page 3, where you will begin your paper.

All the formatting that you need is now in place, and you can begin writing your paper. Below, you will find topics that continue to guide your writing in the body of your paper including: organizing your writing, headings, in text citations, and the dreaded reference page! Of course, feel free to navigate other resources in this book as you need them.

Page 3 - The Main Body

Now that your title page and abstract are correctly formatted, you can begin focusing on writing your paper. Because each paper is unique and requires unique formatting based on the information in the paper, I will outline some general rules to follow in the body of your paper below as they appear chronologically in most papers.

The Introduction:

• *Never* use the word "Introduction" in a heading. The body of all APA papers should begin centered and at the top of page 3 (if not using an abstract, start at the top of page 2). Repeat the title of your paper at the top of page three before you start writing.

SLAVERY AND THE CIVIL WAR   3

Slavery and the Civil War

Once you have typed the title of your paper and centered it, you can begin writing the

introduction. Be sure to indent each time you begin a new paragraph.

- The introduction to your paper is your paper's first impression to the reader. Don't be afraid to be witty and funny, but always avoid sarcasm in your writing.

- The introduction should always include a thesis, or a statement about what you plan to accomplish in your paper. It's okay to simply say, "In this paper, I will..." however, if you feel you can be more creative with your thesis, there is no wrong way to write it so long as it is clear and concise.

- The structure of your introduction and thesis should be built to mirror the rest of your paper. Thus, if you have a certain order of topics in your introduction, the same order should be followed in your paper.

- Pay special attention to transition sentences. Transition sentences should be used anytime your paper changes subjects or direction. Their job is to close a topic you've just discussed and introduce the next topic. Transition sentences add a seamless quality to your writing and help carry the reader easily through your writing.

- Your introduction should be proportional to the rest of your paper. For a 3 - 5 page paper, your introduction should only be 5 - 7 sentences. For longer papers, your introduction can be more extensive. In the case of writing a book, introductions can take up multiple paragraphs, if not the entire first chapter.

The Body of Your Paper:

- The body of your paper contains the collection of your research. All major points should be brought up here, not in the introduction or the conclusion.

- Build an outline before writing your paper, then stick to it!

- Be okay with writing a rough draft of your paper. I know it seems like a waste of time, but as college professor, I can tell which students spent time writing their papers and which students threw them together at the last minute.

- The body of your paper should always be working toward fulfilling the thesis (what you've set out to do) as stated in the introduction.

- The first sentence of each paragraph should be a good summary of what the whole paragraph is going to address. The last sentence should be a transition out of the current topic and a brief introduction into the next topic. If you are not necessarily changing topics from one paragraph to the next, a transition is not necessary.

- Most quotations require a page number or paragraph number. For more see *quotations.*

- Decide at the beginning of your paper whether you are going to use one or two spaces after a period. Both are correct, just remain consistent throughout your paper.

- Personal communication is given an in text citation but not included on the reference page. See *What Counts as Personal Communication?*

- If an electronic resource does not have a page number, reference the paragraph number using the abbreviation "para."

- The indentations of a block quotation match the tab indent and are double spaced. When using a block quote, do not use quotation marks.

- You may use tables to explain information in your paper. However, tables should not be included in the body of your paper. Rather, they go on their own page (one table per page) after your Reference page.

The Conclusion:

- The main point to having a conclusion is to tie up the paper in a nice pink bow. Okay, maybe not pink. But, think of the introduction and conclusion as bookends to the body of your paper. No new substantial information should be included in your conclusion.

- The conclusion should answer the question, "Did I accomplish what I said I would accomplish in my thesis?".

- It is appropriate for the conclusion to mirror the introduction, though it is not necessary.

- Just as with your introduction, be creative when writing your conclusion. Try incorporating a piece of poetry, a stanza of a song, or a phrase from a popular speech. Using artistic elements in your writing will add a new dimension to your writing.

Headings:

After building an outline for our paper, if we choose to do so stylistically, we can turn the subtitles in our outline into proper 1st, 2nd, and 3rd order headings in our APA paper. We don't want an entire sentence for a subtitle, but rather just a few words that capture the essence of this segment of our paper. Here we are using a first order heading (in this case, let's call our first order heading: Social Tensions of Slavery).

- Note that we would *never* use "Introduction" as a heading.

It is common to have a second heading but rare to have third order headings in an undergraduate paper. However, they become more common as papers become longer and more sophisticated, as in graduate level work. In case you need them, here is how each of them should look in your paper:

54

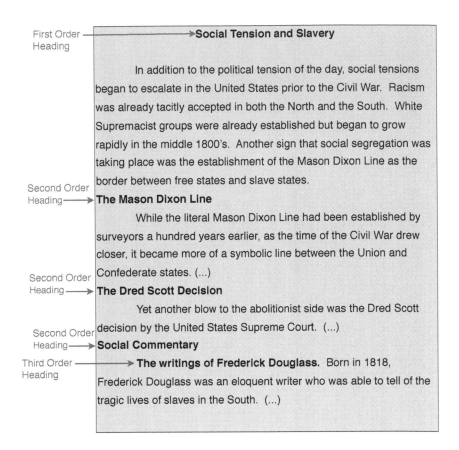

First Order Heading → **Social Tension and Slavery**

In addition to the political tension of the day, social tensions began to escalate in the United States prior to the Civil War. Racism was already tacitly accepted in both the North and the South. White Supremacist groups were already established but began to grow rapidly in the middle 1800's. Another sign that social segregation was taking place was the establishment of the Mason Dixon Line as the border between free states and slave states.

Second Order Heading → **The Mason Dixon Line**

While the literal Mason Dixon Line had been established by surveyors a hundred years earlier, as the time of the Civil War drew closer, it became more of a symbolic line between the Union and Confederate states. (...)

Second Order Heading → **The Dred Scott Decision**

Yet another blow to the abolitionist side was the Dred Scott decision by the United States Supreme Court. (...)

Second Order Heading → **Social Commentary**

Third Order Heading → **The writings of Frederick Douglass.** Born in 1818, Frederick Douglass was an eloquent writer who was able to tell of the tragic lives of slaves in the South. (...)

Here is another way to remember how to format headings in your APA paper:

Heading Rules	1st Order Heading	2nd Order Heading	3rd Order Heading	4th Order Heading	5th Order Heading
Placement	Centered	Left Justified	*Left Justified and Indented*	*Left Justified and Indented*	*Left Justified and Indented*
Bold?	Yes	Yes	Yes	Yes	No
Capitalization	The first letter of all essential words capitalized	The first letter of all essential words capitalized	Only the first word in the subtitle and any proper names should be capitalized	Only the first word in the subtitle and any proper names should be capitalized	Only the first word in the subtitle and any proper names should be capitalized
Spacing	Press "return" button once afterward	Press "return" button once afterward	Do not press the "return" button. End with a period.	Do not press the "return" button. End with a period.	Do not press the "return" button. End with a period.

In Text Citations and Quotations:

- Any time you quote any source, you must enclose the entire quote, word for word, in quotation marks (" "). If there is an error in the original quote, you still must quote it word for word but include *[sic]* (make sure to italicize) at the end of the sentence.

- Block quotations are used for any quotation longer than 40 words. The APA Manual describes very specific rules that apply to block quotes.

  - Block quotes start and end on their own lines. They do not share lines with other information in your paper.
  - The every line of the block quotation is indented a half inch.
  - As with the rest of an APA formatted paper, the block quote is double spaced.
  - Block quotes do not have quotation marks around them.
  - Punctuation after a block quote goes before the in-text citation.

General Rules for In Text Citations:

- If you are citing an entire book or publication, the in text citation includes the authors last name and year of publication: (Anders, 2013).

- If you are citing a specific page or paragraph in a publication: (Anders, 2013, p. 14). For a paragraph: (Anders, 2013, para. 14).

In-text Quoting a Website Article:

- After your quote, in parenthesis include the authors last name, the year of the publication, the title of the article, and the paragraph where you obtained the quote.

(Jones, 2011, History of the Civil War, para. 5).

- On all quotations, the period that completes the sentence goes to the outside of the closed parenthesis.

In-text Quoting a Book with one Author:

- If you choose to include the author's name as part of the sentence, write the authors name, then in parenthesis write the year of the publication. After the quote, in parenthesis write the page number with the period on the outside of the closed parenthesis. Here is how it should look:

    Smith (2011) says, "For those slaves who were obedient, life was still difficult" (p. 113).

- If you don't mention the authors name in the sentence, write the author's last name, date of publication, and page number in parenthesis.

    "For those slaves who were obedient, life was still difficult" (Smith, 2011, p. 113).

- For paraphrased material, simply include the authors last name and the date of publication:

    (Smith, 2011).

- Or for two authors enter them in the order that they appear on the book with the publication year following:

  (Anderson and Ziegler, 2009).

- Any time you use direct quotations you must include a page number (for books) or paragraph numbers (websites) for your in text citations.

- For Personal Communication that is not written, do not use paragraph or page numbers as a part of a direct quotation.

In-text Quoting a Book with Two Authors:

- Include both last names of each author in the order that they appear on the book with the date of the publication and page number.
- For dual authors, use the word "and" in between the authors.

  (Anderson and Ziegler, 2009, p. 104).

- If the authors have the same last name, go alphabetically by their first initial.

  (A. Anderson and B. Anderson, 2009, p. 104).

In-text Quoting a Source with 3 to 5 Authors (as often with textbooks)

- The *first time* you use this source, include each authors' last name in the order they appear on the cover with the date of publication and the page number. Here is what it should look like:

  (Anderson, Beiler, Johnson, and Smith, 2001, p. 47).

- After the first quote, if you use this source again, simply write:

  (Anderson, et al., 2001, p. 59).

- If there are more than six authors, use the first authors' name with et al. for every citation.

In-text Quoting When No Author is Listed:

- If no author is credited for a book or website, cite the organization name associated with the work. For example:

  (American Psychological Association, 2009, p. 11).

Religious Texts

- Citing the Bible or other religious texts can be confusing. Here is the general format for your in-text citations. Immediately after a biblical quote: (*Version of the Bible*, Abbreviation of Biblical book. verse start-verse end).

  (i.e.: *Complete Jewish Bible,* Gen. 11.6-12.8).

  As long the version of the bible stays the same in future in-text citations, for any subsequent quotes, simply cite the biblical book, chapter and verse. (Gen. 11.6-12.8).

Punctuation:

We have already addressed punctuation to some degree, however here are some things to keep in mind:

- There should always be two spaces after any punctuation that ends a sentence.

- Every letter beginning a sentence should be capitalized along with any proper names.

- When citing a source in the body of your paper, place the period after the in-text citation parenthesis.

References and the Reference Page:

If there is any part of APA formatting that students struggle with the most, it is their reference sheet. After much weeping and gnashing of teeth, I have decided to organize the reference section of this book in the order that the references are built - from left to right.

Formatting Note: One limitation in producing a book like this is formatting hanging indents. In APA format, all references that are longer than the first line should be indented and double spaced. I recognize that the examples throughout this book do not follow that format. Always be sure to indent the second, third, etc. lines of your references.

- **Author and Editor Names**
- **Date of Publication**
- **Name of Article (if needed)**
- **Title of Reference**
- **Location**
- **Name of Publisher**

In this section, I will explain each section of an APA reference in more detail than you probably care to read - but it's there if you need it. If you wish to skip all the explanations and look directly at samples for over 30 references, skip to the completed references examples given at the end of this section. If you would like a more visual representation of the same information below, visit my website, where I am compiling examples of all kinds APA references.

Formatting Author and Editor Names:

With a few exceptions, the first thing we write when referencing a resources is the author or editor names. The author or authors last name is written first with a comma, then their first initial with a period. For example an author with the name John Anders would be written like this:

Anders, J.

For two authors, the same practice works by writing their names in the order they appear in the book (usually alphabetical, but not necessarily) - separating the names with an ampersand (&). For example:

Anders, J. & Bieler, R.

For three to seven authors:

List the authors by last name, separating each name with a comma. When you get to the last author, place an ampersand (&) symbol *before* their name. For example:

Anders, J., Bieler, R., Johnson, L., & White, B.

If you are using a book that has an editor or editors, their names are used in this section as well. For a single editor, follow the author formula above and simply add (Ed.). or (Eds.). after the editor's first name initial. For example:

Anders, J. (Ed.).

For multiple editors:

Anders, J. & Bieler, R. (Eds.).
Anders, J., Bieler, R., Johnson, L., & White, B. (Eds.).

For publications that list corporations, organizations, governments as the author, write the organization name as it is printed *without* abbreviating any part of the name. For example:

Department of Education. (2013). *The education in America.* Salem: OR. Anchor Press.

Specifically, for publications classified as Online Encyclopedias, Journal Article with No Author, and Magazine Article with No Author, the name of the article is placed where the author name would usually go. For example, the full reference for an online encyclopedia would look like this:

Speed of Light. (n.d.). In *The Encyclopedia Britannica* (Vol. 8, pp. 218-219). Retrieved from http://www.encyclopediabrittanica.com.
Formatting the Date of Publication:

The date of publication is placed after the author or editor name. When formatting our references for the date of publication, we will primarily use three different formats - depending on the kind of reference. Regardless of the format, the date of publication is always placed inside of parentheses.

The *most common* format for the date of publication is the year of publication inside of a parenthesis. This is how it will appear next to an author's name:

    Anders, J. (2013).

Use this format for the following references:

- Book with One Author
- Book with Multiple Authors
- Edited Book with No Authors
- Edited Book with an Author or Authors
- Edition of Book Other than the First Edition
- Multivolume Work
- Encyclopedia Entry
- E-book (if a date of publication is given)
- Online Encyclopedia
- Online Lecture Notes and Presentation Slides
- Web Page
- Computer Software
- Journal Article
- Journal Article with no Author (if a date of publication is given)
- Chapter from an Online Article or E-book

Another way to format the date of publication is to insert the year of publication, then the month and date. As compared with the references above which are more traditional, this format is primarily used for references related to articles or blog posts. For example, a newspaper article reference would look like this:

Anders, J. (2013, May 6). APA rules. *The Denver Post.* Retrieved from http://www.denverpost.com

Notice how both the year and the month and day are written. Use this format for the following references:

- Newspaper Article
- Blog
- Audio Podcast
- Online Forum or Discussion Board
- Online Magazine Article
- Magazine Article with No Author
- Online Book Reviews

Finally, (n.d.). stands for no date, is used in cases where a reference does not have a date of publication associated with it. This format can be used for any reference, though it is most commonly used for online references since publication dates for online articles are not always listed. Here is an example of how this would look for an E-book with no publication date listed:

Anders, J. (n.d.). *APA made easy.* Retrieved from http://www.apamadeeasy.com

If you can find a publication date, you should use it. If you cannot find a publication date, use (n.d.). in this field.

Formatting the Name of Article (If Needed)

If the reference you are citing an article, the name of the article should be a part of your reference. The name of the article follows the date of publication and precedes the title of the publication. Format the name of the article by capitalizing only the first letter of the first word in the name of the article. For example, if we were to cite a Podcast that has an episode name and title, it would look like this:

Anders, J. (2013, May 6). APA rules. Podcast retrieved from http://www.APAMadeEasy.edu/podcast.htm

Of course, this is APA format, it can't be that easy! There are other additions that go in the article field in addition to the article name. Notably, when citing computer hardware, your article field will include: [computer software] in brackets. For example:

Anders, J. (2013). APA rules [computer software]. New York, NY: Anchor Press.

For a blog post:

Anders, J. (2013, May 6). APA rules [Web log comment]. Retrieved from http://www.youversustheworld.com/references

Title of Reference

If the resource you are referencing does not have an article name, the title of the publication will appear after the date of publication. In APA format the title of a publication is always *italicized.*

Special Note on Capitalization: One mistake I see students make surrounds the concept of capitalization. You will notice in the example below that certain titles are capitalized and others are not. Here are the criteria to use when deciding whether or not to capitalize a title:

- Always capitalize all essential words in a journal title.
- Only the first letter of the first word is capitalized when when writing titles for books, articles, chapters, and web pages. If you are referencing a sub-title, capitalize the first letter of the first word as well.
- Proper nouns are *always* capitalized, even in the titles for books, article, chapters, and webpages. A proper noun is a name for a person, place, thing, or idea.
- The first letter of the first word after a colon or dash can be capitalized.

Here is an itemized way of thinking about writing the title of each kind of reference:

Books, E-books, and Newspaper Articles: Simply list and italicize the title of the publication. Only the first letter of the first word is capitalized.

Books with Editions Other than the First: List and italicize the name of the book and write the number of the edition in parentheses.

APA made easy (4th ed.).

A Multivolume Work: List and italicize the title of the reference and write the volume(s) that you used in your paper in parentheses. If you have page numbers available, include them within the parenthesis as well. For a single volume use (Vol.) and for multiple volumes use (Vols.).

APA made easy (Vol. 2).
APA made easy (Vols. 1-3).

For an Encyclopedia Entry or Online Encyclopedia Entry: Write "*In the*" then the encyclopedia title. For example, "In *The Encyclopedia Britannica.*" In parentheses include the volume number(s) and the page numbers that you are referencing. In this particular title, the word "In" is not italicized, nor are the volume and page numbers.

In *The Encyclopedia Britannica* (Vol. 4, pp. 36-85).
In *The Encyclopedia Britannica* online.

Online Lecture Notes and/or Presentation Slides: Italicize the title of the lecture and in brackets note the kind of presentation noted.

APA Made Easy [Powerpoint Document].

Audio Podcast: Italicize and write the title of the Podcast. Afterward, we would write "Podcast retrieved from ..."

APA Made Easy. Podcast Retrieved from http://www.itunes.com

Journals, Online Journals, and Journals with no Author: Journals are the anomaly in the reference page. First, we capitalize all essential words. Our first example will be of a journal with an italicized volume number and unitalicized page numbers only:

APA Made Easy, 12, p. 25.

If the journal you are citing has an volume and issue number, the issue number goes after the volume number, unitalicized and in parentheses:

APA Made Easy, 12(4), pp. 15-33.

Magazine Article, Online Magazine Article, Magazine Article with no Author: The title section for a magazine article looks a lot like a journal as it includes the volume and issue numbers, if noted in the magazine. After the volume and or the issue number, the unitalicized page numbers of the reference are included.

For a magazine with a volume number only:

APA Made Easy Magazine, 14, 28-31.

The title of a magazine with a volume number and issue number:

APA Made Easy Magazine, 14(8), 28-31.

Location of Publication

The location section of the reference page notes either where the reference was published (City and State), the website that the reference was published, or a DOI. Because of the popularity of online research, DOI's are becoming increasingly popular. Always include a DOI at the end of your reference if possible.

The standard location for most physical reference materials includes the city and state initial where the reference was published. A comma is entered after the city name and before the state initial. After the state initial include a colon. For example:

New York, NY:

This location format is typical for the following types of references:

- Book with One Author
- Book with Multiple Authors
- Edited Book with No Authors
- Edited Book with an Author or Authors
- Edition of Book Other than the First Edition
- Multivolume Work
- Encyclopedia Entry
- Computer Software

For resources based online, this section of our reference is used to denote where we retrieved the resource from. Typically, we start these location references with the words "Retrieved from". For example, if we are referencing a blog, we write:

Retrieved from http://www.youversustheworld.com/blog

Publisher

For print resources, the publisher is the last section of the reference! Simply list the publisher one space after the colon of the state initial. Write it exactly as it is written in the resource you are referencing and add a period at the end and you are done!

Putting It All Together: Examples of Completed References and In Text Citations

Below are numerous examples of both references and in-text citations for various scenarios. Under each category is an example of the full reference for your reference page followed by various ways to write an in text citation based on a paraphrase or direct quote of the material.

Book with One Author:

Reference Example:

Author Last Name, First Name. First Initial. (Year of Publication). *Title of publication.* City, State Initials of Publication: Publisher.

Anders, J. (2012). *APA made easy.* New York, NY: Anchor Press.

In text citations for Book with One Author:

Example #1: Paraphrase
According to Anders (2012), writing in APA format can be easy.

Example #2: Paraphrase
With so many resources available, writing in APA format can be easy (Anders, 2012).

Example #3: Direct Quote
Anders (2012) stated, "Writing in APA format can be easy" (p. iv).
More Reference Examples of Books with One Author:

Book with One Author, Standard Date of Publication
Anders, J. (2012). APA made easy. New York, NY: Anchor Press.

Book with One Author, No Date
Anders, J. (n.d.). APA made easy. New York, NY: Anchor Press.

Book with One Author, Republished Date - Use the latest date listed
Anders, J. (2012). APA made easy. New York, NY: Anchor Press.

In Text Citation Example - Cite both the original published date and the date of the republished version: (Anders, 2000/2014).

Book with One Author, Edition Other Than First
Anders, J. (2012). APA made easy (4th ed.). New York, NY: Anchor Press.

Book with One Author, Revised Edition
Anders, J. (2012). APA made easy (Rev. ed.). New York, NY: Anchor Press.

Book with One Author, Title with Subtitle
Anders, J. (2012). APA made easy: Writing with style. New York, NY: Anchor Press.

Book with One Author, No Date, Title with Subtitle
Anders, J. (n.d.). APA made easy: Writing with style. New York, NY: Anchor Press.

Book with One Author, Title with Proper Noun
Anders, J. (2014). The life and times of J. Edgar Hoover. New York, NY: Anchor Press.

Book with One Author with Hyphenated Name
Anders, J. -R. (2014). The life and times of J. Edgar Hoover. New York, NY: Anchor Press.

Book with One Author, Title with Subtitle, Edition Other than First
Anders, J. (2014). APA made easy: Writing with style (4th ed.). New York, NY: Anchor Press.

Book with One Author, No Date, Title with Subtitle, Edition Other than First
Anders, J. (n.d.). APA made easy: Writing with style (4th ed.). New York, NY: Anchor Press.

Book with One Author, Title with Series
Anders, J. (2012). APA made easy: Vol. 4. Writing with style. New York, NY: Anchor Press.

Book with One Author, Ebook or Electronic Version
Anders, J. R. (2014). Writing with style. Retrieved from http://www.apamadeasy.com/ebooks

Book with One Author, No Date, Ebook or Electronic Version
Anders, J. R. (n.d.). Writing with style. Retrieved from http://www.apamadeasy.com/ebooks

Book with One Author, Ebook or Electronic Version, with DOI
Anders, J. R. (2014). Writing with style. doi:10.1234567890

Book with Two Authors:

Reference Example:

First Author Last Name, First Author Initials., & Second Author Last Name, Second Author Initials. (Year of Publication). *Title of Publication.* City, State Initials: Publisher.

Anders, J., & Bieler, R. (2012). *APA made easy.* New York, NY: Anchor Press.

In text citations for a Book with Two Authors:

Example #1: Paraphrase
There have been cases where people have compared Anders and Bielers's book (2012) to *APA Made Easy* because of the similarities in writing style.

Example #2: Paraphrase
Easy APA Formatting (Anders & Bieler, 2012) has been compared to APA Made Easy.

Example #3: Direct Quote

The book on Fairy Tales was described as "a wonderful tale of hope and dreams" (Anders & Bieler, 2012, p. 155).

More Reference Examples of Books with Two Authors

Book with Two Authors, Standard Date of Publication
Anders, J., & Beiler, R. (2012). APA made easy. New York, NY: Anchor Press.

Book with Two Authors, No Date
Anders, J., & Beiler, R. (n.d.). APA made easy. New York, NY: Anchor Press.

Book with Two Authors, Republished Date - Use the latest date listed
Anders, J., & Beiler, R. (2012). APA made easy. New York, NY: Anchor Press.

In Text Citation Example - Cite both the original published date and the date of the republished version: (Anders & Beiler, 2000/2014).

Book with Two Authors, Edition Other Than First
Anders, J., & Beiler, R. (2012). APA made easy (4th ed.). New York, NY: Anchor Press.

Book with Two Authors, Revised Edition
Anders, J., & Beiler, R. (2012). APA made easy (Rev. ed.). New York, NY: Anchor Press.

Book with Two Authors, Title with Subtitle
Anders, J., & Beiler, R. (2012). APA made easy: Writing with style. New York, NY: Anchor Press.

Book with Two Authors, No Date, Title with Subtitle
Anders, J., & Beiler, R. (n.d.). APA made easy: Writing with style. New York, NY: Anchor Press.

Book with Two Authors, Title with Proper Noun
Anders, J., & Beiler, R. (2014). The life and times of J. Edgar Hoover. New York, NY: Anchor Press.

Book with Two Authors with Hyphenated Name
Anders, J.-R., & Beiler, R. (2014). The life and times of J. Edgar Hoover. New York, NY: Anchor Press.

Book with Two Authors, Title with Subtitle, Edition Other than First
Anders, J., & Beiler, R. (2014). APA made easy: Writing with style (4th ed.). New York, NY: Anchor Press.

Book with Two Authors, No Date, Title with Subtitle, Edition Other than First
Anders, J., & Beiler, R. (n.d.). APA made easy: Writing with style (4th ed.). New York, NY: Anchor Press.

Book with Two Authors, Title with Series
Anders, J., & Beiler, R. (2012). APA made easy: Vol. 4. Writing with style. New York, NY: Anchor Press.

Book with Two Authors, Ebook or Electronic Version
Anders, J. T., & Beiler, R. M. (2014). Writing with style. Retrieved from http://www.apamadeasy.com/ebooks

Book with Two Authors, No Date, Ebook or Electronic Version
Anders, J. T., & Beiler, R. M. (n.d.). Writing with style. Retrieved from http://www.apamadeasy.com/ebooks

Book with Two Authors, Ebook or Electronic Version, with DOI
Anders, J. T., & Beiler, R. M. (2014). Writing with style. doi:10.1234567890

Book with Three to Five Authors

Reference Example:

Last Name, First Initial., Second Last Name, First Initial., & Third Last Name, Third First Initial. (Date of Publication). *Title of work.* Location City, State Initial: Publisher.

Smith, C. A., Johnson, F., & Zeigler, R. A. (2013). *APA made easy* . New York, NY: Anchor Press.

In Text Citation Examples:

Follows the same as the above book format except:

For your first time citing a book with three authors, your in text citation should appear like this:

(Smith, Johnson, & Zeigler, 2013)

For subsequent citations after the first:

(Creston et al., 2013)

More References Examples with Three to Five Authors

Book with Three Authors, Standard Date of Publication
Anders, J., Smith, D. R., & Rohn, R. (2012). APA made easy. New York, NY: Anchor Press.

Book with Three Authors, No Date
Anders, J., Smith, D. R., & Rohn, R. (n.d.). APA made easy. New York, NY: Anchor Press.

Book with Three Authors, Republished Date - Use the latest date listed
Anders, J., Smith, D. R., & Rohn, R. (2012). APA made easy. New York, NY: Anchor Press.

In Text Citation Example - Cite both the original published date and the date of the republished version: (Anders, Smith, & Robin, 2000/2012).

Book with Four Authors, Edition Other Than First
Anders, J., Rossier, R. A., Swarinski, H., & Peters, B. (2012). APA made easy (4th ed.). New York, NY: Anchor Press.

Book with Four Authors, Revised Edition
Anders, J., Rossier, R. A., Swarinski, H., & Peters, B. (2012). APA made easy (Rev. ed.). New York, NY: Anchor Press.

Book with Four Authors, Title with Subtitle
Anders, J., Rossier, R. A., Swarinski, H., & Peters, B. (2012). APA made easy: Writing with style. New York, NY: Anchor Press.

Book with Five Authors, Title with Proper Noun
Beuregaard, S. P., Hume, D. A., Spinoza, B., Plantinga, A., & Craig, W. L. (2014). The life and times of J. Edgar Hoover. New York, NY: Anchor Press.

Book with Five Authors with Hyphenated Name
Anders, J.-R., Hume, D. A., Spinoza, B., Plantinga, A., & Craig, W. L. (2014). The life and times of J. Edgar Hoover. New York, NY: Anchor Press.

Book with Five Authors, Title with Subtitle, Edition Other than First
Beuregaard, S. P., Hume, D. A., Spinoza, B., Plantinga, A., & Craig, W. L. (2014). APA made easy: Writing with style (4th ed.). New York, NY: Anchor Press.

Book with Five Authors, No Date, Title with Subtitle, Edition Other than First
Beuregaard, S. P., Hume, D. A., Spinoza, B., Plantinga, A., & Craig, W. L. (n.d.). APA made easy: Writing with style (4th ed.). New York, NY: Anchor Press.

Book with Five Authors, Ebook or Electronic Version
Beuregaard, S. P., Hume, D. A., Spinoza, B., Plantinga, A., & Craig, W. L. (2014). Writing with style. Retrieved from http://www.apamadeasy.com/ebooks

Book with Five Authors, No Date, Ebook or Electronic Version
Beuregaard, S. P., Hume, D. A., Spinoza, B., Plantinga, A., & Craig, W. L. (n.d.). Writing with style. Retrieved from http://www.apamadeasy.com/ebooks

Book with Five Authors, Ebook or Electronic Version, with DOI
Beuregaard, S. P., Hume, D. A., Spinoza, B., Plantinga, A., & Craig, W. L. (2014). Writing with style. doi:10.1234567890

Book with Six to Seven Authors

Reference Example:

Creston, J. P., Anders, R. F., Wilson, D. A., Peters, B. O., Roberts, M. A., Mathers, Y. O., & Nehman, T. (2013). *Hiking in the forest.* New York, NY: Anchor Press.

In Text Citation Example:

Follow the format for all in text citations with six to seven authors:

(Creston et al., 2013)

More Reference Examples With Six to Seven Authors

Book with Six Authors, Standard Date of Publication
Creston, J. P., Anders, R. F., Wilson, D. A., Peters, B. O., Roberts, M. A., & Nehman, T. (2012). APA made easy. New York, NY: Anchor Press.

Book with Six Authors, No Date
Creston, J. P., Anders, R. F., Wilson, D. A., Peters, B. O., Roberts, M. A., & Nehman, T. (n.d.). APA made easy. New York, NY: Anchor Press.

Book with Six Authors, Republished Date - Use the latest date listed
Creston, J. P., Anders, R. F., Wilson, D. A., Peters, B. O., Roberts, M. A., & Nehman, T. (2012). APA made easy. New York, NY: Anchor Press.

In Text Citation Example - Cite both the original published date and the date of the republished version: (Creston et al., 2000/2012).

Book with Six Authors, Edition Other Than First
Creston, J. P., Anders, R. F., Wilson, D. A., Peters, B. O., Roberts, M. A., & Nehman, T. (2012). APA made easy (4th ed.). New York, NY: Anchor Press.

Book with Six Authors, Revised Edition
Creston, J. P., Anders, R. F., Wilson, D. A., Peters, B. O., Roberts, M. A., & Nehman, T. (2012). APA made easy (Rev. ed.). New York, NY: Anchor Press.

Book with Seven Authors, Ebook or Electronic Version
Whitters, M. J., Crossen, J. D., Matthews, P., Homes, R., Keller, J. R., Moreland, J. P., & Lorenzen, S. (2014). Writing with style. Retrieved from http://www.apamadeasy.com/ebooks

Book with Seven Authors, No Date, Ebook or Electronic Version
Whitters, M. J., Crossen, J. D., Matthews, P., Homes, R., Keller, J. R., Moreland, J. P., & Lorenzen, S. (n.d.). Writing with style. Retrieved from http://www.apamadeasy.com/ebooks

Book with Seven Authors, Ebook or Electronic Version, with DOI
Whitters, M. J., Crossen, J. D., Matthews, P., Homes, R., Keller, J. R., Moreland, J. P., & Lorenzen, S. (2014). Writing with style. doi: 10.1234567890

<u>Book with Eight or More Authors</u>

Reference Example:

Creston, J. P., Anders, R. F., Wilson, D. A., Peters, B. O., Roberts, M. A., Mathers, Y. O., . . . Nehman, T. (2013). *Cooking for dummies.* New York, NY: Anchor Press.

Note: When referencing 8 or more authors, the first six authors are listed than an ellipse (. . .) and then the final author's name.

In Text Citation Example:

Using an in-text citation for a book with eight or more authors always looks like this:

(Creston et al., 2013)

More References Examples for Books with Eight or More Authors

Book with Eight or More Authors, Standard Date of Publication
Creston, J. P., Anders, R. F., Wilson, D. A., Peters, B. O., Roberts, M. A., Mathers, Y. O., . . .Nehman, T. (2012). APA made easy. New York, NY: Anchor Press.

Book with Eight or More Authors, No Date
Creston, J. P., Anders, R. F., Wilson, D. A., Peters, B. O., Roberts, M. A., Mathers, Y. O., . . .Nehman, T. (n.d.). APA made easy. New York, NY: Anchor Press.

Book with Eight or More Authors, Republished Date - Use the latest date listed
Creston, J. P., Anders, R. F., Wilson, D. A., Peters, B. O., Roberts, M. A., Mathers, Y. O., . . .Nehman, T. (2012). APA made easy. New York, NY: Anchor Press.

In Text Citation Example - Cite both the original published date and the date of the republished version: (Whitters et al., 2000/2012).

Book with Eight or More Authors, Edition Other Than First
Creston, J. P., Anders, R. F., Wilson, D. A., Peters, B. O., Roberts, M. A., Mathers, Y. O., . . .Nehman, T. (2012). APA made easy (4th ed.). New York, NY: Anchor Press.

Book with Eight or More Authors, Revised Edition
Creston, J. P., Anders, R. F., Wilson, D. A., Peters, B. O., Roberts, M. A., Mathers, Y. O., . . .Nehman, T. (2012). APA made easy (Rev. ed.). New York, NY: Anchor Press.

Book with Eight or More Authors, Title with Subtitle
Creston, J. P., Anders, R. F., Wilson, D. A., Peters, B. O., Roberts, M. A., Mathers, Y. O., . . .Nehman, T. (2012). APA made easy: Writing with style. New York, NY: Anchor Press.

Book with Eight or More Authors, No Date, Title with Subtitle
Creston, J. P., Anders, R. F., Wilson, D. A., Peters, B. O., Roberts, M. A., Mathers, Y. O., . . .Nehman, T. (n.d.). APA made easy: Writing with style. New York, NY: Anchor Press.

Book with Eight or More Authors, Title with Proper Noun
Creston, J. P., Anders, R. F., Wilson, D. A., Peters, B. O., Roberts, M. A., Mathers, Y. O., . . .Nehman, T. (2014). The life and times of J. Edgar Hoover. New York, NY: Anchor Press.

Book with Eight or More Authors, Title with Subtitle, Edition Other than First
Creston, J. P., Anders, R. F., Wilson, D. A., Peters, B. O., Roberts, M. A., Mathers, Y. O., . . .Nehman, T. (2014). APA made easy: Writing with style (4th ed.). New York, NY: Anchor Press.

Book with Eight or More Authors, No Date, Title with Subtitle, Edition Other than First
Creston, J. P., Anders, R. F., Wilson, D. A., Peters, B. O., Roberts, M. A., Mathers, Y. O., . . .Nehman, T. (n.d.). APA made easy: Writing with style (4th ed.). New York, NY: AnchorPress.

Book with Eight or More Authors, Title with Series
Creston, J. P., Anders, R. F., Wilson, D. A., Peters, B. O., Roberts, M. A., Mathers, Y. O., . . .Nehman, T. (2012). APA made easy: Vol. 4. Writing with style. New York, NY: Anchor Press.

<u>Edited Book, No Author:</u>

Reference Example:

Editor Last Name, First Initial. (Ed.). (Year of Publication). *Title of Publication.* City, State Initials: Publisher.

With One Editor, No Author
Anders, J. (Ed.). (2013). *APA made easy.* New York, NY: Anchor Press

With Two Editors, No Author
Anders, J., & Beiler, R. (Eds.). (2012). *APA made easy.* New York, NY: Anchor Press.

With Three Editors, No Author
Anders, J., Beiler, R., & Markol, C.A. (Eds.). *APA made easy.* New York, NY: Anchor Press.

In text citation for Edited Book:

Example #1: Paraphrase
Anders and Baker (2012) demonstrated how easy writing in APA format can be.

Example #2: Direct Quote
As stated in Anders and Beiler (2012), "Writing in APA Format is easy when you have the right tools" (p. 77).

More Examples:

One Editor, No Date, No Author
Anders, J. (Ed.). (n.d.). APA made easy. New York, NY: Anchor Press.

One Editor, No Author, Republished Version - Use the latest date listed
Anders, J. (Ed.). (2014). APA made easy. New York, NY: Anchor Press.

In Text Citation Example - Cite both the original published date and the date of the republished version: (Anders, 2000/2014).

One Editor, No Author, Edition Other Than First
Anders, J. (Ed.). (2013). APA made easy (4th ed.). New York, NY: Anchor Press.

One Editor, No Author, Revised Edition
Anders, J. (Ed.). (2013). APA made easy (Rev. ed.). New York, NY: Anchor Press.

One Editor, No Author, Title with Subtitle
Anders, J. (Ed.). (2013). APA made easy: Writing with style. New York, NY: Anchor Press.

One Editor, No Author, No Date, Title with Subtitle
Anders, J. (Ed.). (n.d.). APA made easy: Writing with style. New York, NY: Anchor Press.

One Editor, No Author, Title with Subtitle, Edition Other Than First
Anders, J. (Ed.). (2013). APA made easy: Writing with style (4th ed.). New York, NY: Anchor Press.

One Editor, No Author, Title with Series
Anders, J. (Ed.). (2013). APA made easy: Vol. 4. Writing with style. New York, NY: Anchor Press.

With Two Editors, No Author
Anders, J., & Beiler, R. (Eds.). (2012). *APA made easy.* New York, NY: Anchor Press.

More Examples:

Two Editors, No Date, No Author
Anders, J., & Markol, C. A. (Eds.). (n.d.). APA made easy. New York, NY: Anchor Press.

Two Editors, No Author, Republished Version - Use the latest date listed
Anders, J., & Markol, C. A. (Eds.). (2014). APA made easy. New York, NY: Anchor Press.

In Text Citation Example - Cite both the original published date and the date of the republished version: (Anders & Markol, 2000/2014).

Two Editors, No Author, Edition Other Than First
Anders, J., & Markol, C. A. (Eds.). (2013). APA made easy (4th ed.). New York, NY: Anchor Press.

Two Editors, No Author, Revised Edition
Anders, J., & Markol, C. A. (Eds.). (2013). APA made easy (Rev. ed.). New York, NY: Anchor Press.

Two Editors, No Author, Title with Subtitle
Anders, J., & Markol, C. A. (Eds.). (2013). APA made easy: Writing with style. New York, NY: Anchor Press.

Two Editors, No Author, No Date, Title with Subtitle
Anders, J., & Markol, C. A. (Eds.). (n.d.). APA made easy: Writing with style. New York, NY: Anchor Press.

Two Editors, No Author, Title with Subtitle, Edition Other Than First
Anders, J., & Markol, C. A. (Eds.). (2013). APA made easy: Writing with style (4th ed.). New York, NY: Anchor Press.

With Three Editors, No Author
Anders, J., Beiler, R., & Markol, C.A. (Eds.). *APA made easy.* New York, NY: Anchor Press.

More Examples:

Three Editors, Standard Date, No Author
Anders, J., Beiler, R., & Markol, C.A. (Eds.). (2013). APA made easy. New York, NY: Anchor Press.

Three Editors, No Date, No Author
Anders, J., Beiler, R., & Markol, C.A. (Eds.). (n.d.). APA made easy. New York, NY: Anchor Press.

Three Editors, No Author, Republished Version - Use the latest date listed
Anders, J., Beiler, R., & Markol, C.A. (Eds.). (2014). APA made easy. New York, NY: Anchor Press.

In Text Citation Example - Cite both the original published date and the date of the republished version: (Anders, Beiler, & Markol, 2000/2014).

Three Editors, No Author, Edition Other Than First
Anders, J., Beiler, R., & Markol, C.A. (Eds.). (2013). APA made easy (4th ed.). New York, NY: Anchor Press.

Three Editors, No Author, Revised Edition
Anders, J., Beiler, R., & Markol, C.A. (Eds.). (2013). APA made easy (Rev. ed.). New York, NY: Anchor Press.

Three Editors, No Author, Title with Subtitle
Anders, J., Beiler, R., & Markol, C.A. (Eds.). (2013). APA made easy: Writing with style. New York, NY: Anchor Press.

Three Editors, No Author, No Date, Title with Subtitle
Anders, J., Beiler, R., & Markol, C.A. (Eds.). (n.d.). APA made easy: Writing with style. New York, NY: Anchor Press.

Three Editors, No Author, Title with Subtitle, Edition Other Than First
Anders, J., Beiler, R., & Markol, C.A. (Eds.). (2013). APA made easy: Writing with style (4th ed.). New York, NY: Anchor Press.

Edited Book with an Author or Authors:

Reference Example:

Author Last Name, First Initials. (Date of Publication). *Title of Publication, (Ed.).* City, State Initials: Publisher.

Anders, J. (2012). *APA made easy, (Ed.).* New York, NY: Anchor Press.

In text citations for Edited Book with Author or Authors:

Example #1: Paraphrase
Anders and Bieler (2012) claim that the sixth edition of the APA Manual is better than its predecessor.

Example #2: Paraphrase
Writing in APA has never been easier (Anders & Bieler, 2012).

Example #3: Direct Quote
Writing in APA has "never been easier" (Anders & Bieler, 2012, p. 12).

More Examples:

Edited Book with One Author, Standard Date
Anders, J. (2012). Headings in APA. In S. Johnson (Ed.), APA made easy (pp. 95-97). New York, NY: Anchor Press.

Edited Book with One Author, No Date
Anders, J. (n.d.). Headings in APA. In S. Johnson (Ed.), APA made easy (pp. 95-97). New York, NY: Anchor Press.

Edited Book with One Author, Republished Date - Use latest date listed
Anders, J. (2012). In S. Johnson (Ed.). APA made easy (p. 95). New York, NY: Anchor Press.

In Text Citation Example - Cite both the original published date and the date of the republished version: (Anders, 2000/2014).

Edited Book with One Author, Edition Other Than First
Anders, J. (2012). Headings in APA. In S. Johnson (Ed.), APA made easy (3rd ed., pp. 95-97). New York, NY: Anchor Press.

Edited Book with One Author, Series Editor
Anders, J. (2012). Headings in APA. In S. Johnson (Series Ed.), APA made easy (pp. 95-97). New York, NY: Anchor Press.

Edited Book with One Author, Revised Edition
Anders, J. (2012). Headings in APA. In S. Johnson (Ed.), APA made easy (Rev. ed., pp. 95-97). New York, NY: Anchor Press.

Edited Book with One Author, Title with Subtitle
Anders, J. (2012). Headings in APA. In S. Johnson (Ed.), APA made easy: An important step in formatting (pp. 95-97). New York, NY: Anchor Press.

Edited Book with One Author, No Date, Title with Subtitle
Anders, J. (n.d.). Headings in APA. In S. Johnson (Ed.), APA made easy: An important step in formatting (pp. 95-97). New York, NY: Anchor Press.

Edited Book with One Author, Title with Proper Noun
Anders, J. R. (2014). In S. Johnson (Ed.). The life and times of J. Edgar Hoover (pp. 103-105). New York, NY: Anchor Press.

Book without an Author or Editor

Reference Example:

Title of book (Edition number, if needed). (Date of Publication). City, State Initials: Publisher.

APA made easy. (2013). Denver, CO: Anchor Press.

In Text Citation Example:

(APA Made Easy, 2013).

More Examples:

Book without an Author, Standard Date
APA made easy. (2013). Denver, CO: Anchor Press.

Book without an Author or Editor, No Date
APA made easy. (n.d.). Denver, CO: Anchor Press.

In Text Citation Example:
(APA Made Easy, n.d.)

Book without an Author or Editor, Edition Other than First
APA made easy (4th ed.). (2013). Denver, CO: Anchor Press.

Book without an Author or Editor, Revised Edition
APA made easy (Rev. ed.). (2013). Denver, CO: Anchor Press.

Book without an Author or Editor, Title with Subtitle
APA made easy: Writing with style. (2012). New York, NY: Anchor Press.

In Text Citation:
(APA Made Easy, 2012)

Book without an Author or Editor, No Date, Title with Subtitle
APA made easy: Writing with style. (n.d.). New York, NY: Anchor Press.

In Text Citation:
(APA Made Easy, n.d.)

Book without an Author or Editor, Title with Series Name
APA made easy: Vol. 4. Writing with style. (2012). New York, NY: Anchor Press.

Book with an Edition Other than First:

Reference Example:

Authors Last Name, First Initial. (Date of Publication). *Title of Publication* (Edition Number.). City, State Initials: Publisher.

Anders, J. (2012). *APA made easy* (4th ed.). New York, NY: Anchor Press.

Editions are not mentioned specifically for in text citations. Use criteria such as the type of reference (book, website, etc.) for your in text citation.

Multivolume Work:

Reference Example:

Author's Last Name, First Initial. (Year of Publication). *Title of Publication* (Volume number). City, State Initials: Publisher.

Anders, J. (2012). *APA made easy* (Vols. 1-3). New York, NY: Anchor Press.

In text citation for Multivolume Work:

Example #1: Paraphrase
According to Anders (2012), writing in APA format can be easy.

Example #2: Paraphrase (with more than one author)
Easy APA Formatting (Anders & Bieler, 2012) has been compared to *APA Made Easy.*

Example #3: Direct Quote
As stated in Anders and Beiler (2012), "Writing in APA Format is easy when you have the right tools" (p. 77).

Printed Encyclopedia Entry:

Reference Example:

Author's Last Name, First Initials. (Year of Publication). In *The Name of the Encyclopedia* (Volume number, page(s) number).

Anders, J. (2012). APA rules. In *Encyclopedia Britannica* (Vol. 14, pp. 332-335). New York, NY: Anchor Press.

In text citation for Encyclopedia Entry:

If an encyclopedia entry has an author, follow the format for a book with one author or an edited book.

Example #1: Paraphrase (no author)
The *Encyclopedia Britannica* describes *B.F. Skinner* (2012) as an American psychologist and proponent of Behaviourism.

Example #2: Direct Quote (no author)
B.F. Skinner (2012) was "a successful psychologist who espoused the concept of psychological Behaviouralism" (p. 233).

Online Encyclopedia with Author:

Reference Example:

Author Last Name, First Initials. (Year of Publication). Article title. In *Name of Encyclopedia Website* (Volume number, page numbers). Retrieved from URL

Anders, J. (2013). APA rules. In *The Encyclopedia Britannica* (Vol. 7, p. 15). Retrieved from http://www.encyclopediabritannica.com

Online Encyclopedia without an Author:

Reference Example:

Article title. (Date of Publication). In *Name of Encyclopedia Website* (Volume number, page numbers). Retrieved from URL

APA rules. (n.d.). In *Encyclopedia Britannica (Vol. 8, pp. 218-219).* Retrieved from http://www.encyclopediabrittanica.com

In text citation for Online Encyclopedia Entry:

Example #1: Paraphrase (no author)
The *Encyclopedia Britannica* describes *B.F. Skinner* (n.d.), as an American psychologist and proponent of Behaviourism.

Example #2: Direct Quote (no author)
He was "a successful psychologist who espoused the concept of psychological Behaviouralism" ("B.F. Skinner," n.d.).

Note: (n.d.) stands for "No Date". If you find a date associated with an entry, you should use it in the place of (n.d.).

Newspaper Article:

Reference Example:

Author Last Name, First Initials. (Year, Date of Publication). Article title. *Newspaper title,* page numbers.

Anders, J. (2013). APA rules. *The Denver Post,* pp. A2, B4.

Online Newspaper Article:

Reference Example:

Author Last Name, First Initials. (Year, Date of Publication). Article title. *Title of Publication.* Retrieved from URL

Anders, J. (2012, May 6). APA rules. *The Denver Post*. Retrieved from http://www.denverpost.com

In text citation for Newspapers, Journal Articles, and Periodicals:

Example 1: Paraphrase
Anders (2012) believed that APA format was the best way to organize a research paper.

Example #2: Paraphrase
While APA formatting is helpful, not everyone likes using it (Anders, 2012).

Example #3: Direct Quote
According to Anders (2012), "APA formatting is helpful when writing a research paper" (p. 45).

E-books:

Reference Example:

Author Last Name, First Initials. (Year of Publication). *Title of publication* [Kindle Edition]. Retrieved from http://www.amazon.com

Anders, J. (n.d.). *APA made easy* [Kindle Edition]. Retrieved from http://www.ibooks.com

In text citations for E-books or Electronic Course Textbook:

Example #1: Paraphrase
According to Anders (2012), finding regular times to write will reduce the stress level for college students.

Example #2: Paraphrase
Finding regular writing times throughout the week will reduce stress levels in college students (Anders, 2012).

Example #3: Direct Quote
In order to reduce levels of stress, "college students should schedule regular writing times throughout the week" (Anders, 2012, p. 9).

More Examples:

One Editor, No Author, Electronic Book/Ebook
Anders, J. A. (Ed.). (2014). Writing with style. Retrieved from http://
www.youversustheworld.com/ebookreferences

One Editor, No Author, Chapter in Electronic Book/Ebook
We format for fun. (2014). In R. Miller (Ed.), Writing with style (pp. 91-103).
Retrieved from http://www.youversustheworld/bookchapter

Book with One Author, Ebook or Electronic Version, with DOI
Anders, J. R. (2014). Writing with style. doi:10.1234567890

Chapter in Electronic Book/Ebook with One Author
Anders, J. A. (2014). Writing in style. In R. Miller (Ed.), Writing Fundamentals (pp.
93-103). Retrieved from http://www.youversustheworld.com/chapterreferences

Chapter in Electronic Book/Ebook with One Author, Title with Subtitle
Anders, J. (2012). Writing in style. In R. Miller (Ed.), APA made easy: A new way
of formatting. Retrieved from http://www.youversustheworld.com/
chapterreferences

Personal Communication (requires In-text Citation only)

Content that cannot be recovered by another Individual is often considered
personal communication. Personal communication may be things like
emails, phone calls, personal interviews, lectures, skype calls, etc.

For your personal communication here are the two different kinds of
citations:

Example #1:
P. M. Novak (personal communication, February 21, 2013) Insert the
quote or paraphrased material.

Example #2:
Quote/paraphrase material (P. M. Novak, personal communication,
February 21, 2013).

Online Lecture Notes and Presentation Slides:

Reference Example:

Anders, J. (2012). *APA Made Easy* [Powerpoint document]. Retrieved from Lecture Notes Online Website: http://www.easteregg.edu/classes/phil201

In text citations for Online Lecture Notes, Syllabi, and other Supplemental Documents:

Example #1: Supplemental Documents, Syllabi, or Lecture Notes
According to the University of Notre Dame Five Week Review (2012), students should check in with their advisors.

Example #2: Powerpoint Slides as Presentation (in classroom)
According to the Powerpoint presentation in HUM 130 (2012), Buddhism believes that the Four Noble Truths are the way to eliminate suffering.

> *If you have obtained the name of the presenter or professor, use their first initial and last name as part of your reference with "personal communication" and date of the presentation:* (J. Anders, personal communication, August 3, 2012).

Example #3: Powerpoint Slides (online)

The Federal Government's ability to fix problems in the education system seem ineffective (Federal Education Right to Privacy, 2012).

According to the Powerpoint presentation from the Federal Education Right to Privacy Act (2012), "Teachers are to keep each students' grades confidential" (slide 6).

Website:

Reference Example:

Website with Author

Author Last Name, First Initials. (Year of Publication). *Title of website.* Retrieved from URL

Anders, J. (2012). APA rules. Retrieved from http://www.denverpost.com

Website without Author

Title of website. (Year of Publication). Retrieved from URL

In text citations for web pages with or without an author:

Example #1 (with an author; paraphrase)

According to Anders (2012), writing in APA format is an easy way to organize a research paper.

Example #2 (with an author; direct quote)

Anders (2012) stated, "Writing in APA format is an easy way to organize a research paper" (APA Rules, para. 3).

Example #3 (no author)

> *Note: if no author is available, the APA asks that we use the name of the organization, corporation, agency, etc.*

Writing in APA is really easy when we have the tools that we need (National Writers Association, 2012).

Example #4: (no author, direct quote)
The National Writers Association (2012) notes, "Writing in APA format is easy when we have all the tools we need" (Research Writing: APA, para. 4).

Computer Software:

Reference Example:

Author Last Name, First Initials. (Year of Publication). Title of software [computer software]. City, State Initials: Publisher.

Anders, J. (2012). APA rules [computer software]. New York, NY: Anchor Press.

In text citation for Computer Software:

Note: When using computer software as a reference, be sure to include the version number in your In text citation.

Example #1: Paraphrase
The numerical evidence (see Figure 5) is displayed in a Microsoft Excel spreadsheet (Version 10.2).

Blog:

Anders, J. (2012, May 6). APA rules [Web log comment]. Retrieved from http://www.youversustheworld.com/blog

In text citations for a Blog will follow the same format as a Website (see above).

Podcast:

Reference Example:

Author Last Name, First Initial. (Year, Date of Publication). Name of publication [Episode Number]. *Title of Podcast.* Podcast retrieved from URL

Anders, J. (2012, May 6). APA rules [Episode 10]. *APA Made Easy.* Podcast retrieved from http://www.youversustheworld.com/podcast.htm

In text citations for Podcasts:

Example #1: Paraphrase
In Matkovich's (2012) podcast about APA formatting, he discusses easy ways to remember how to reference podcasts.

Example #2: Paraphrase
This podcast discusses various ways to cite web sites and print media (Matkovich, 2012).

Online Forum or Discussion Board:

Reference Example:

Author Last Name, First Initials. (Year, Date of Publication). Title of the message [Message number]. Message posted to URL

Anders, J. (2012, May 6). APA rules [Msg. 17]. Message posted to http://www.groups.yahoo.com/forum

In text citations for Online Forum Messages and Discussion Boards:

Example #1: Paraphrase
In Anders's (2012) Week Seven forum message, he states, "APA formatting simply requires too much time to be practical" (para. 2).

Example #2: Paraphrase
In response to the Week Seven forum message, the professor asked the students to discuss the major difference between Christianity and Judaism (Anders, 2012).

Journal Article:

Reference Example:

Author Last Name, First Initials. (Year of Publication). Title of journal article. *Name of Journal, Volume Number* (Issue Number if needed), page numbers.

Anders, J. (2013). APA rules. *APA Made Easy, 17,* 188-194.

Example with Issue Number and DOI:
Anders, J. (2013). APA rules. *APA Made Easy, 17*(2), 188-194. doi: 10.86462.

In text citation for Journal Article:

Example #1: Paraphrase
Anders (2012) thinks that classes in research writing do not improve the writing quality of college students.

Example #2: Paraphrase
Research writing classes have not been effective in improving the overall writing quality in college students (Anders, 2012).

Example #3: Direct Quote
In his review, Anders (2012) claims that, "writing in APA format helps students think logically about their subject matter" (p. 122).

Journal Article with no Author:

Reference Example:

Article Title. (Year of Publication). *Name of Journal, Volume Number*(Issue number if needed), Page Numbers. doi: 10.xxxxx.

APA Rules. (2012). *APA Made Easy, 17*(2), 188-194. 10.86462.

In text citations for Journal Article with No Author:

Note: Titles of shorter works should be placed in italics

Example #1: Paraphrase
The "Business" section (2012) of *Popular News* magazine shows an increase of the unemployment rate in America.

Example #2: Paraphrase
Popular News magazine highlighted the increase of unemployment in America ("Business," 2012).

Magazine Article:

Reference Example:

Author Last Name, First Initials. (Year, Date of Publication). Article title. *Name of Magazine, Volume Number,* page numbers.

Anders, J. (2013, May 6). APA rules. *APA Made Easy Magazine, 32,* 16-19.

Online Magazine Article:

Reference Example:

Author Last Name, First Initials. (Year, Month of Publication). Article title. *Title of Magazine,* Page numbers. Retrieved from URL

Anders, J. (2012, May). APA rules. *APA Made Easy,* 14. Retrieved from http://www.youversustheworld.com

In text citations of Online Magazine Articles follow the same format as Journal Articles (see above).

Magazine Article with no Author:

Reference Example:

Name of article. (Year, Month of Publication). *Title of Publication, Volume Number,* Page Numbers.

APA rules. (2012, May). *APA Made Easy, 14,* 90-92.

In text citations of Online Magazine Articles with no Author follow the same format as Journal Articles with no Author (see above).

In Print Chapter:

Reference Example:

Author Last Name, First Initial. (Year of Publication). Title of section. In *Title of Publication* (page numbers). City, State Initials: Publisher.

Anders, J. (2013). APA rules. In *APA Made Easy* (p. 67). New York: NY: Anchor Press.

Chapter from Online Article or E-book Chapter:

Reference Example:

Authors Last Name, First Initials. (Year of Publication). Name of article. In *Name of Publication* (Edition Number). Retrieved from URL

Anders, J. (2012). APA rules. In *APA Made Easy* (14). Retrieved from http://www.denverpost.com
In text citations for Online Article or E-book Chapter:

Example #1: Paraphrase
Anders (2012, Chapter 14) gives us good reasons to follow APA formatting.

Example #2: Direct Quote
As stated by Anders (2012, APA Made Easy), "Every APA formatted paper should include a title page" (p. 21).

Chapter from a Book with an Editor Only:

Reference Example:

Chapter Author Last Name, First Initials. (Year of Publication). Name of the chapter. In Editor's First Initials Last Name (Ed.), *Title of publication* (page numbers). City, State Initials: Publisher.

Anders, J. (2013). APA rules. In R. Seiple (Ed.), *Formatting for professionals* (pp. 67-88). New York, NY: Anchor Press.

Social Media

General Template
Author Last name, First Initial. [Screen name]. (Date). Title of post: link to post [Type of post]. Retrieved from http://www.nameofwebsite.com

Example:

JAnders. (2014, May 6). Description of post content: http://shorturlifpossible.com [Tweet]. Retrieved from http://www.twitter.com

In text citations differ depending on the website and the type of post. Generally, Twitter posts will look like this:

(Matkovich, 2011) or (Last name, Year of Post)

Facebook:
(Last name, Year of Post).

If post is a company, (Ameritrade, 2011)

Examples:

Twitter Update/Tweet, Author's Name Known
Anders, J. [JAnders]. (2014, May 6). Description of post content: http:// shorturlifpossible [Tweet]. Retrieved from http://www.twitter.com

Twitter Update/Tweet, Author's Name Known, No Date
Anders, J. [JAnders]. (n.d.). Description of post content: http://
shorturlifpossible [Tweet]. Retrieved from http://www.twitter.com

Twitter Update/Tweet, Author's Name Unknown (Use Screen Name)
JAnders. (2014, May 6). Description of post content: http://
shorturlifpossible.com [Tweet]. Retrieved from http://www.twitter.com

Twitter Update/Tweet, Author's Name Unknown (Use Screen Name),
Date Reasonably Guessed
JAnders. (ca. 2014). Description of post content: http://
shorturlifpossible.com [Tweet]. Retrieved from http://www.twitter.com

Twitter Update/Tweet, Author's Name as Company or Corporation
United Parcel Service. (2014, May 6). Description of post content: http://
shorturlifpossible [Tweet]. Retrieved from http://www.twitter.com

Multiple Twitter Updates/Tweets from Same Author or Organization
JAnders. (2014a). Alphabetize by title and add letter after date http://
shorturlifpossible.com [Tweet]. Retrieved from http://www.twitter.com

JAnders. (2014b). Be sure to alphabetize by title and add letter after date :
http://shorturlifpossible.com [Tweet]. Retrieved from http://www.twitter.com

Facebook Examples:

Facebook Status Update, Author's Name Known
Anders, J. [John]. (2014, May 6). Write out status update here [Facebook
status update]. Retrieved from https://www.facebook.com/APAMadeEasy?
ref=hl

Facebook Page, Author's Name Known
Anders, J. [John]. (2014, May 6). Write out status update here [Facebook
page]. Retrieved from https://www.facebook.com/APAMadeEasy?ref=hl

Facebook Note, Author's Name Known
Anders, J. [John]. (2014, May 6). Write out status update here [Facebook
note]. Retrieved from https://www.facebook.com/APAMadeEasy?ref=hl

Facebook Status Update, Author's Name Known, No Date
Anders, J. [John]. (n.d.). Write out status update here [Facebook status update]. Retrievedfrom https://www.facebook.com/APAMadeEasy?ref=hl

Facebook Status Update, Author's Name Unknown (Use Screen Name)
JAnders. (2014, May 6). Write out status update here [Facebook status update]. Retrieved from https://www.facebook.com/APAMadeEasy?ref=hl

Facebook Status Update, Author as Company or Corporation
APA Made Easy. (2014, May 6). Write out status update here [Facebook status update]. Retrieved from https://www.facebook.com/APAMadeEasy?ref=hl

Facebook Status Update, Author as Company or Corporation, Date Reasonably Guessed
APA Made Easy. (ca. 2014). Write out status update here [Facebook status update].Retrieved from https://www.facebook.com/APAMadeEasy?ref=hl

Multiple Facebook Status Updates from Same Author or Organization
JAnders. (2014a). Alphabetize by title and add letter after date: http://shorturlifpossible.com [Facebook status update]. Retrieved from http://www.facebook.com.com/apamadeeasy

JAnders. (2014b). Be sure to alphabetize by title and add letter after date : http://shorturlifpossible.com [Facebook status update]. Retrieved from http://www.facebook.com/apamadeeasy

In text citations for more than one post:
(JAnders, 2014a)
(JAnders, 2014b)

Comment on Facebook Status Update - See Personal Communication Section

Facebook Application
Farmersville. (2014). Fake farming [Facebook application]. Retrieved from http://apps.facebook.com/fakefarming

Online Book Reviews:

Reference Example:

Authors Last Name, First Initials. (Year, Date of Publication). Name of review [Review of the book *Name of the Book*]. *Name of Publication.* Retrieved from URL

Anders, J. (2012, May 6). APA rules [Review of the book *APA Made Easy*]. *The Denver Post.* Retrieved from http://www.denverpost.com

In text citations for Book Reviews follow the medium (website, book, journal, etc.) from which it was pulled.

A Quick Note about DOI's (Digital Object Identifiers)

Due to the sudden rise of academic digital resources, doi's are now recommended by the APA Manual. Essentially, doi's were created to help provide a consistent and steady location for things such as digital media, academic articles, etc. This is especially important because referenced links used in a research paper often become broken links over time. The doi is the best way to ensure that the resources you used online can be accessed, be it today or ten years from now.
So, how do you reference a resource with a doi? I am glad you asked! Right now, many online journal articles will simply include the doi in their listing.

Example of Journal Article Reference:

Author last name, First initial. Middle initial. (Publication year). Title of Article. *Title of journal. Vol. number* (Issue number), Page number starts-ends. Document Object Identifier.

Here's how it will look in the real world:

Anders, J. (2012). APA Rules. *Journal of Boring Things, 17*(2), 168-173. doi: 10.1037/a0016089.

Tips on using DOI's:

- Because the use of DOI's are new, there is no customary place where they are listed from resource to resource. Thus, you may have to look around to find them. In some cases they are found in the database citation information for the article. In other cases they can be found on the title page of the article while other times it can be found as a footnote.

- If you don't see a DOI, use the APA rule to cite an electronic source without a DOI. If you can find a DOI for your resource, always put it at the end of your reference on your reference page.

- DOI's always start with the number 10.

- To find a citation of a resource by its DOI, go to www.doi.org or www.crossref.org.

Checklist for the Reference Page

- Your reference page should be on its own page, separate from the text of your paper.

- The word "References" should be written at the top of the page (do not italicize, bold, underline, or use quotations).

- The reference page should be set to double spaced as with the rest of your paper.

- Use only 1 space in between all punctuation in your reference page.

- When citing a source, the first line should not be indented. If your citation falls onto a second or third line, those lines should be indented by hitting the tab key once, or by spacing in 1/2 of an inch. (This is referred to as a hanging indentation).

- All proper names including the titles of books, author names, companies, etc. should be capitalized.

- Only the **first letter** of the title of your reference should be capitalized for web pages, books, chapters, and articles. The only time the first letter should be capitalized in a title is when it includes a proper name or for any journal article (i.e. *APA made easy*). The same rule applies to subtitles (i.e. *APA made easy: Formatting your paper for professional writing*).

- Only spell out the authors' last name. Their first name and middle initial use only the first letter.

- For references with multiple authors, always keep the order the same as they are listed on the publication.

- If you are referencing multiple pages, use "pp.". If you are only citing one page use "p.". The only time you should not use this is with regards to referencing Magazine Articles.

- Make sure to include any source that you assigned an in-text citation in the body of your paper.

- The APA warns against using Wiki's as a resource for any scholarly paper. Before using a wiki reference, check with your instructor.

- Email correspondence is not included in your reference sheet. If you quote an email in your paper, cite the source after the quote: (J. Anders, personal communication, May 6, 2012).

- If you quote the Bible or a religious text in your paper, the proper reference should look like this:

  Complete NIV Bible. Ed. Bill Johnson. New York: Baker House, 2012. Print.

- Your references should include enough detailed information so that the reader can find the source on their own if they wish.

- For two or more authors, be sure to make use of the ampersand (&) before the name of the last author.

- Book references always begin with the Authors Last Name followed by their first initial and middle initial. However, if the book does not have a stated author or editor, then the reference begins with with the title of the book in italics.

- Never use a period after a doi number or URL in a reference.

What Should I Italicize on My Reference Page?

If you have ever tried to build a reference page with different types of references, trying to remember what to italicize is nearly impossible! Below, you will find a list of when it is appropriate to italicize a section of your reference.

- Author and Editor Names of books are never italicized.
- The Date of Publication is never italicized
- Article titles are not italicized
- Titles of Books, E-books, Encyclopedias, Newspapers, Presentations, Websites, Dissertations, and Podcasts *are italicized.*
    - Websites that have no author listed are referenced by placing the title of the website where the author name usually goes. In that case, the title of the website is not italicized.
- When referencing a Journal or Magazine, the name of the journal or magazine and the volume number *are italicized.* The issue numbers and page numbers are not italicized.

Endless Variations

After all that information, I must humbly admit that I have only touched the proverbial surface of all the reference possibilities. My goal here is keep this book considerably smaller than the APA Manual, thus I cannot give a full treatment of all references - and I don't imagine you would be too interested in reading it either! Thus, in this spirit of humility, if I have not answered your question, and you cannot find the answer in the reference section of my website, write and let me know. I will get back to you within 24 hours with an answer.

Using Tables, Figures and Appendices

Tables:

The APA discourages the use of tables and graphs unless absolutely necessary. If you decide that you need a table, stay APA compliant by following the rules listed below:

- The first table that you use at the end of your paper should be called "Table 1", followed by "Table 2", and so forth. The title (Table 1) is left justified and placed right under the running header.

- As with the rest of your paper, all text in tables should be 12 font in Times New Roman.

- A table should include its own title; something short but clear representing what the table is about, italicized and presented with each essential word capitalized. For example: *Statistical Variance of Behavior Between Teenagers and Young Adults.*

- Each table gets its own page. Do not put more than one table on a page.

- Horizontal lines can be used in APA tables to separate information, though vertical lines in between information is not permitted.

- As with the rest of your paper, all elements of the table should be double spaced.

- If you decide to include tables, they should be referenced in the text of the paper. Tables are not supposed to be used as "stand alone" illustrations if they are not explained in the body of your paper.

- Tables should be last, after your reference list and appendixes.

Table Headings:

- Table headings should be right justified.

- The first letter of each heading should be capitalized.

- Each column in your table should include a heading that describes the information therein.

- You may abbreviate standard terms within your discipline, which are common knowledge without further explanation. Definitions not common to the industry should be explained underneath the table starting with the word *Note.* which is italicized.

Using an Appendix:

There are not too many steadfast rules about how to format an Appendix (other than those that you would use in your APA paper already).

- Each appendix uses its own page. Thus if you have more than one, each should go on a new page.

- The first Appendix is simply titled "Appendix". Any additional Appendices go in alphabetical order (Appendix A, B, C,...).

- The first line is indented 5 – 7 spaces.

Bullet Points and Lists

Any time you wish to separate points of your paper, you can use bullet points. They should be indented (most word processors do this automatically) and not begin with capital unless you start with a Proper Noun (the name of a person, country, etc.) or the beginning of a new sentence. As always, make sure they are double spaced.

For lists that require a chronological or hierarchical order, such as instructions or linear steps, use numerals with a period after them. For example: 1. 2. 3.
As with the bullet points, they should be indented and double spaced.

APA Quick Checklist

The Title Page:

- Insert "Running head: YOUR TITLE IN ALL CAPS" as a header in the upper left hand corner of the page.
- Insert the page number as a header in the upper right hand corner of the page.
- All margins should be 1 inch.
- The title of the paper, with all the essential words capitalized should be 10 spaces (or 5 double spaces) from the header at the top of the page.

- Insert the date that the paper was completed 2 spaces (1 double space) after the date of the paper.
- Insert the university or institution for which the paper was written 2 spaces (1 double space) after the date of the paper.
- Other information may be added to the title page at the discretion of your instructor.
- The APA recommends Times New Roman font with 12 font for all papers, though Arial font may be used.

The Abstract Page:

- Abstracts are rare for undergraduate papers. Check with your instructor to see if they require an abstract for the papers in your course.
- The short title of your paper should be in the upper left hand header without the words, "Running head:" which only appear on the title page.
- Your abstract should always be on page 2. Check to make sure your abstract coincides with the second page of your paper. If you are not using an abstract, the body of your paper begins on page 2.
- Do not indent your abstract as you would the paragraphs in the body of your paper.
- Your abstract should only be between 200 - 250 words in length. This may increase depending on the size of your paper. If you feel that your paper is long enough to warrant a longer abstract, be sure to get the approval of your instructor.
- Once you complete your abstract, begin a new page for the body of your paper. Your abstract should not share a page with any other part of your paper.

The Body of Your Paper:

- The body of your paper should begin on page 3 if you are including an abstract, or on page 2 if you are not including an abstract.
- The short title of your paper should be in the upper left hand header of the page.
- If you begin your paper with a heading, it should be centered on the page, boldfaced, though not underlined. Never use the word "Introduction" as a subtitle in an APA paper.
- Second order headings are in bold, but justified to the left margin and stand on a line of their own.

- Third order headings are in bold, justified to the left margin but indented (press Tab once) and need a period at the end. The first sentence of your paragraph immediately follows the third order heading without pressing "Return".
- All punctuation that ends a sentence requires two spaces afterward to start a new sentence. (*Note - there is some debate over whether APA requires two spaces after a period or only one. The APA Manual is silent on the issue, though for a draft, it requires two spaces after a period.)
- Every quote should include quotation marks and an in-text citation afterward in parenthesis.
- All paraphrasing of previously published material needs an in-text citation with the authors last name and year of publication separated by a comma.
- All in-text citations should be enclosed in parentheses.
- All in-text citations should correlate to a reference on your reference page.

The Reference Page:

- Your reference page should be the last page of your document unless you are using a table or appendices.
- Your reference page should be its own page, not shared with any part of the body of your paper.
- The word "References" should be centered at the top of the page (do not bold, italicize, underline, or use quotations marks).
- The first line of any reference should be left justified with no indentation. If your references spill over onto additional lines, they should all be indented (press tab once).

How to Organize Your Paper:

There are 3 main parts to your paper: 1) Introduction 2) Body 3) Conclusion. After teaching writing for a number of years to students, here is some practical advice to help you organize your paper.

- **Build an Outline.** An outline will give you a "big picture" of what you are going to accomplish and how you plan to organize the research in your paper. Let's take a look at a sample outline.

- **Create a Title:** Believe it or not, titles are something that college students often give very little thought to. However, think of them as your paper's first impression. You may want it to be funny, witty, or clever. No matter what you decide, make sure your paper's title really hits at the center of the topics covered in your paper.

- **Develop a Thesis:** A thesis is a sentence or two that describes what you plan to accomplish in your paper. Without a thesis, your paper will lack direction and clarity. Let's say we are writing a paper on the Civil War and Slavery. Here is a sample of a possible thesis for our outline:

Title: Slavery and the Civil War

- Thesis: In this paper, I will explore the political, social, and economic effects of the Civil War on Slavery.

Notice that the writer makes it clear what they want to accomplish in this paper. While a thesis can be stated in a number of ways, the goal is to provide the reader with the direction and clarity. The rest of the paper should be written around this goal.

After you come up with a great thesis, you can begin working on the body of your paper. The body of your paper should follow the *order* of your thesis. For example, because the first issue mentioned in my thesis is the political effects of the Civil War on Slavery, the first topic should address the political effects on slavery.

Title: Slavery and the Civil War

*- Thesis: In this paper, I will explore the **political**, social, and economic effects of the Civil War on Slavery.*

*I. The United States was very divided **politically** on the topic of slavery prior to the Civil War*

A great tip to bring clarity to your paper is the use of subtitles. It helps break the paper down into smaller pieces all of which guide the reader through your paper for effortless reading.

Just remember, the shorter your paper, the less subtitles that are needed. For example, in a 3 page paper, no more than 2-3 subtitles should be used. In a 5 page paper, no more than 5-7 subtitles should be used. The subtitles should be pulled from the major points of your paper. We will talk about this more once we complete our outline.

Once you are done with your first major point (I), fill in the details from your research on the political effects of slavery using second order subtitles (A,B,C):

Title: Slavery and the Civil War

- Thesis: In this paper, I will explore the political, social, and economic effects of the Civil War on Slavery.

I.   The United States was very divided politically on the topic of slavery prior to the Civil War.

A. The North: While those in the North held slaves, it was the South that used slaves to the greatest degree. The North was made up of abolitionists who sought to end slavery.
B. The South: The South favored the holding of slaves which were purchased at auction by southern land owners.
C. Ultimately, the political division between the North and South caused the southern states to succeed from the Union.

We will continue to develop our paper in this way. Remember, always follow the flow of your thesis and whenever possible, the smaller points of your paper should be established by the larger flow or context of your paper.

Title: Slavery and the Civil War

*- Thesis: In this paper, I will explore the **political**, **social**, and economic effects of the Civil War on Slavery.*

  I.   *The United States was very divided **politically** on the topic of slavery prior to the Civil War.*

  A. *The North: While those in the North held slaves, it was the South that used slaves to the greatest degree. The North was made up of abolitionists who sought to end slavery.*
  B. *The South: The South favored the holding of slaves which were purchased at auction by southern land owners.*
  C. *Ultimately, the political division between the North and South caused the southern states to succeed from the Union.*

  II. *In addition to the political tensions, the **social** tensions in the United States were very different prior to the Civil War.*

  A. *Socially, the Mason Dixon Line was understood by southern African American slaves as a line of freedom.*
  B. *The Dred Scott decision took away slave rights even north of the Mason Dixon Line.*
  C. *Several popular writings affected the abolitionist movement.*
    1. *The writing of Frederick Douglass emphasized the terrible living conditions of African American slaves.*
    2. *Later, Uncle Tom's Cabin was published with an appeal to Christian ethics against holding slaves.*

Again, notice how the first subtitle (I) of my paper mirrors the first point of my thesis. And, the second subtitle (II) of the second point in my thesis, and so forth.

You will notice that my second section includes sub-points under a subtitle (labeled 1. & 2.). These are called third order subtitles. For the purposes of following the APA, it is important that we know how to format our different subtitles by using the proper headings.

If you have these principles down, your paper will appear organized, well thought out, and clean. Let's look at the rest of the outline:

Title: Slavery and the Civil War

- Thesis: In this paper, I will explore the political, social, and economic effects of the Civil War on Slavery.

I. *The United States was very divided politically on the topic of slavery prior to the Civil War.*
   A. *The North: While those in the North held slaves, it was the South that used slaves to the greatest degree. The North was made up of abolitionists who sought to end slavery.*
   B. *The South: The South favored the holding of slaves which were purchased at auction by southern land owners.*
   C. *Ultimately, the political division between the North and South caused the southern states to succeed from the Union.*
II. *In addition to the political tensions, the social tensions in the United States were very different prior to the Civil War.*
   A. *Socially, the Mason Dixon Line was understood by southern African American slaves as a line of freedom.*
   B. *The Dred Scott decision took away slave rights even north of the Mason Dixon Line.*
   C. *Several popular writings affected the abolitionist movement.*
      1. *The writing of Frederick Douglass emphasized the terrible living conditions of African American slaves.*
      2. *Later, Uncle Tom's Cabin was published with an appeal to Christian ethics against holding slaves.*
III. *Economically, the South had every reason to oppose the abolition of slavery, economically speaking.*
   A. *Slaves were considered owned property. The idea that slaves could be free would amount to southern slave owners losing large amounts of valuable property.*
      1. *See chart on the property value of slaves from 1820 - 1860.*

B. *Heavy commodity industries in the South utilized slave labor to build profits for southern farm owners.*
   1. *Cotton*
   2. *Sugar*
   3. *Oil*

Last but not least, we need to wrap up our paper with a conclusion. Following our previous idea of mirroring the thesis, the conclusion is no different. If the introduction and thesis are telling the reader what we will do in our paper, then the conclusion will tell the reader what we have done (which is hopefully what we said we will do!). Let's look at an example.

Title: Slavery and the Civil War

Thesis: *In this paper, I will explore the* **political, social, and economic** *effects of the Civil War on Slavery.*

IV. Conclusion: In this paper, I have examined the **political, social, and economic** *aspects of slavery in the context of the Civil War. The North and the South were divided politically far before the war began. Moreover, with the Mason Dixon Line drawn, the setting for division between the North and the South became more of a reality. Finally economically the South was not prepared, nor were they in any mood to lose their "property" as the North intended. All of these things were strong precursors to the start of the Civil War.*

As you can see, many of the same elements that made up our thesis and the body of our paper are reflected in our conclusion.

A Few More Paper Writing Tips:

- You may want to wait to write both your Introduction and Conclusion until after your paper is written.

- Always let your thesis guide the rest of your paper.

- Don't feel like you have to title your paper first thing. Often it helps to wait until you have the rest of your paper written first. Be creative!

- Pick a topic that you are interested in. Even if you are writing a paper for a class that you don't particularly like, see if you can incorporate elements of your interest into the subject. For example, let's say you are really interested in history, but you are taking a philosophy course. Perhaps you could write a paper about the culture that a particular philosopher interacted with.

- Everyone has a different writing style. The challenge of writing isn't to do it "right", but to become good at your own style. The APA is just a format or a palette for your writing. Think of your writing as an art and the APA as the frame that you will present your masterpiece!

- Once you have set up your title page, abstract (if you are using one), and have a solid outline, you are in a good position to start writing the body of your paper. Stylistically, the body of the paper is pretty easy. However, there are a few things we need to keep in mind when we are writing. For our purposes, we are going to address the most common elements of a paper written in APA. Specifically: Subtitles, Quotations, In-text citations, and Punctuation.

Formatting Science Papers

Until now we have covered how to write a paper focused on courses in the humanities courses i.e. history or philosophy. However, APA format is also used to write scientific papers such as lab reports. While the principles of APA formatting stay the same, I felt it was necessary to review the format for scientific papers in APA format.

The following sections should be present in an APA formatted lab report *in this order*:

- Title Page (on its own page)
- Abstract (on its own page)
- Introduction (starting on its own page)
- Method
- Results
- Discussion
- References (on their own page)
- Footnotes (not recommended, but allowed - use with caution)
- Tables (if you have them, on their own page)
- Figures (if you have them, on their own page)
- Appendices (if you have them, each on their own page with separate titles)

Let's look at the main sections in order, including any information I haven't covered previously in this book.

Title Page: Your title page will be built exactly the same way we built it in the walkthrough section of this book including 1 inch margins, double spacing, a header, page number, and 12 font type in Times New Roman.

Abstract: Your abstract follows the walkthrough as well. Remember, this is to be a short summary of your entire paper. It's a good idea to wait until your paper is completely written before you write your abstract. And no, don't let the computer build it for you! A well crafted abstract gives a great first impression, so take your time and be concise. I always encourage students to verify the need for an Abstract page with their professor. Some professors expect it, while others do not. Be sure you know what is expected from each professor!

Introduction: Because your Title page and Abstract are on their own pages, your Introduction should start on the third page. Remember, *do not use "Introduction" as your heading.* However, the title of your paper should appear at the top of the page, centered but not in bold. A good way to introduce your topic is to talk about the nature of your research and the problem you are trying to address in your paper. Remember that your introduction should be proportional to the rest of your paper. For example, if your paper is only 5 pages long, one solid paragraph is sufficient. For longer papers, a longer introduction is necessary and thus you may need one or perhaps two pages to properly introduce and set the context for your paper.

Method: (first order heading) This part of your paper should include the heading "Method". Method is a first order heading and thus should be centered, bold, uppercase and lowercase usage. The method portion of your paper can share a page with your introduction, so no need to start a new page. This section is also where you would include:

- **Subjects or Participants:** (second order heading) that you used in your research.
- **Sampling:** (second order heading) including the size of your sample, type of sampling used, etc.
- **Research Design:** (second order heading) includes sufficient details on how your subjects or participants were partitioned into their particular groups.
- **Materials:** (second order heading) which can includes any descriptions of custom material or apparatus that you used in your research.
- **Procedure:** (second order heading) includes things like the instructions given to the participants, the setting of the study, etc.

If you include subsections under these sections, then format them using third order headings and so forth.

Results: (first order heading) follows immediately after the Method section and summarizes the data and tests performed. Remember, this is a scientific paper and your writing should be clear, straightforward, and precise. You will also report statistics in this section.

Discussion: (first order heading) The goal of the discussion section is to pull together all the previous sections, summarize the main findings of your report, and include your interpretation of the data. You should also include conclusions that are justified in light of your own research and previous research. Finally, identify any weaknesses or limitations of your study.

References: (first order heading) As with our walkthrough, your references should be on their own page. Again, be sure to use a hanging indent for any line after the first.

Using Numbers in APA Format:

In the following cases, it is always appropriate to *use words* for numbers:

• If you are using numbers that are 10 and below, they should be presented as words (one, two, three, etc.) i.e. *In this study, we used seven subjects...*

• If you begin a sentence with a number, use words instead of numerics i.e. *Forty-five subjects left the study early...*

• When fractions are used, they should be written in words i.e. *In our study, one-third of the subjects...*

In the following cases, you should always use *numerical values*:

• If you are using numbers that are above 10, they should be presented as numerals (11, 12, 13, etc.) i.e. *In this study, we used 38 subjects...*

• In cases where you are presenting mathematical functions, statistics, or percentages, use numbers i.e. *In this study, 7% of the subjects...*

• Regarding age, points on a scale, or time, use numbers i.e. *8 years old.*

Appendix A: Reference Chart for Common References

Reference	Last Name, First Initial.	(Year of Publication).	*Title of Work.*	Location City, State Initial:	Publisher
Book with 1 Author	Anders, J.	(2012).	*APA made easy.*	New York: NY	Anchor Press.
Book with 2 Author	Anders, J., & Beiler, R.	(2012).	*APA made easy.*	New York: NY	Anchor Press.
Edited Book, No Author	Anders, J., & Beiler, R. (Eds.).	(2012).	*APA made easy.*	New York: NY	Anchor Press.
Edited Book, with an Author	Anders, J.	(2012).	*APA made easy.*	New York: NY	Anchor Press.
Edition Other than First	Anders, J.	(2012).	*APA made easy* (4th ed.).	New York: NY	Anchor Press.
Multivolume Work with Editor	Anders, J. (Ed.).	(2012).	*APA made easy* (Vols. 1-3).	New York: NY	Anchor Press.

Examples taken from above:

Book with One Author:
Anders, J. (2012). *APA made easy.* New York, NY: Anchor Press.

Book with Multiple Authors:
Anders, J., & Bieler, R. (2012). *APA made easy.* New York, NY: Anchor Press.

Edited Book, No Author
Anders, J. & Beiler, R. (Eds.). (2012). *APA made easy.* New York, NY: Anchor Press.

Edited Book with and Author or Authors
Anders, J. (2012). APA made easy. In R. Miller (Ed.), *Easy writing* (p. 97). New York, NY: Anchor Press.

Edition other than First
Anders, J. (2012). *APA made easy* (4th ed.). New York, NY: Anchor Press.

Multivolume Work
Anders, J. (Ed.). (2012). *APA made easy* (Vols. 1-3). New York, NY: Anchor Press.

Appendix B: Reference Chart for New References

Reference	Author Last Name, First Initial.	(Year of Publication).	Name of article.	Title of Work (Vol. and pg. #'s)	Location City, State Initial: or web address.	Publisher.
Encyclopedia Entry	Anders, J.	(2012).	APA rules.	In the *Encyclopedia Britannica* (Vol. 14, pp. 332-335).	New York, NY:	Anchor Press.
Newspaper Article	Anders, J.	(2012, May 6).	APA rules.	*The Denver Post.*	Retrieved from http://www.denverpost.com	
E-books	Anders, J.	(n.d.).		*APA Made Easy.*	Retrieved from http://www.ibooks.com	
Online Encyclopedia*		2. (n.d.).	1. APA rules.	In the *Encyclopedia Britannica* (Vol. 8, pp. 218-219).	Retrieved from http://www.encyclopediabrittanica.com	
Online Lecture Notes and Presentation Slides	Anders, J.	(2012).		*APA Made Easy* [Poworpoint document].	Retrieved from Lecture Notes Online Website: http://www.easteregg.edu/classes/phil201.	
Web Page	Anders, J.	(2012).	APA rules.		Retrieved from http://www.denverpost.com	
Computer Software	Anders, J.	(2012).	APA rules [computer software].		New York, NY:	Anchor Press.
Blog	Anders, J.	(2012, May 6).	APA rules [Web log comment].		Retrieved from http://www.blogger.com/APAMadeEasy.	
Audio Podcast	Anders, J.	(2012, May 6).	APA rules.	*APA Made Easy.*	Podcast retrieved from http://APAMadeEasy.edu/podcast.htm	

Reference	Author Last Name, First Initial.	(Year of Publication).	Name of article.	Title of Work (Vol. and pg. #'s)	Location City, State Initial: or web address.	Publisher.
Online Forum or Discussion Board	Anders, J.	(2012, May 6).	APA rules [Msg. 17].		Message posted to http://www.groups.yahoo.com/forum	
Journal Article	Anders, J.	(2012).	APA Rules.	*APA Made Easy, 17*(2), 188-194.	10.86462.	
Journal Article with no Author		2. (2012).	1. APA Rules.	*APA Made Easy, 17*(2), 188-194.	10.86462.	
Online Magazine Article	Anders, J.	(2012, May).	APA rules.	*APA Made Easy, 14.*		
Magazine Article with no Author		2. (2012, May).	1. APA rules.	*APA Made Easy, 14,* 90-92.		
Chapter from Online article or Ebook Chapter	Anders, J.	(2012).	APA rules.	*In APA Made Easy (14).*	Retrieved from http://www.denverpost.com	
Online Book Reviews	Anders, J.	(2012, May 6).	APA rules.	[Review of the book *APA Made Easy*]. *The Denver Post.*	Retrieved from http://www.denverpost.com	

So Now What? Read this First!

I can see it now, you have in your hands all of the information you need to write flawless papers, effortlessly, as if words simply flow out of you like the wind off the wings of angels! Okay...well, that's probably overstating it. As much as I would love to tell you that writing research papers will now be easier than updating your Facebook status and then wave goodbye to you and your horse as you ride off into a literary sunset - reality is just not that good.

The fact is - writing is hard - *for everyone.* You probably don't believe me. You probably think that there are those people who we love to hate - those who can effortlessly spin tales like the Fairy Godmother making Cinderella's dress. Again, not reality folks. Kurt Vonnegut once said, "When I write, I feel like an armless, legless man with a crayon in his mouth."

I identify more with Walter Wellesley "Red" Smith when he talked about the process of writing in this way: "You simply sit down at the typewriter, open your veins, and bleed."

I used to *hate* it when my instructors would dump a huge research paper on my plate and then have the nerve to say, "No matter what, the most important thing is to have fun with it!" Where do these people come from? That is on par with coffee houses charging 5 bucks for a cup of coffee and then putting the tip jar out to consume any left over change. But I digress.

Even though writing creates a gnawing, grinding feeling inside all of us - you need to know something: *You can do this.* You can write a great paper if you want to. The hardest part is getting started, which is precisely why I wrote this book. I know that if I can help you get started, you will finish the job.

I have also given you access to more materials through my website: www.YouVersusTheWorld. Click on "Extras" at the top of the home page and type: APAFormat (case sensitive) when asked for a password. There you can download some of the materials from this book, a sample Title, Abstract, and Body page for both Word and Pages created by yours truly, and other helpful resources which I want you to have, but were not appropriate to include as a part of this book. Consider them little residual gifts to you as a "thank you" for buying my book. If you would like to see other information added there, write and let me know.

If this book has been helpful to you, and you have a couple extra minutes, I would really appreciate a kind review on the website where you purchased this book (Amazon, iTunes, Barnes and Noble, etc.). I read every review that is written for this book, and I take them very seriously. As you know, we live in a day where ten good reviews carries as much weight as one bad review. Unfortunately, this book does not meet everyone's expectations - and that is okay, though I am extremely grateful for any positive endorsements.

Finally, please know that I wrote this book because I love helping people. Since I published the first version of this book two years ago, I've received emails from Kentucky to the United Kingdom, and now I would love to hear from you. If you have questions, comments, or something that you would like me to include in future versions of this book, don't hesitate to write me directly at Scott@APAMadeEasy.com.

Pura Vida!
Scott Matkovich

About Scott Matkovich

After telling my grandfather that I wanted to be an architect (only because I thought architects made a lot of money), he said to me, "You seem like the kind of person that is better at breaking things down than building things up." Everyone in the room laughed, but it turns out he was right. Once, after watching a Bruce Lee movie, I sat down and sketched all the kicks and punches I could remember from the film. I broke down each of his movements so that I could try to mimic him - admittedly, this often led to self-sustained injuries. Breaking things down in helpful ways has always been my primary approach in writing and teaching. In fact, it's how I wrote this book! I found out, as a teacher, that students didn't want to hear me pontificate on all the things I know. They wanted to learn in a way that they could relate and see how the abstract things I was teaching them mattered in the real world.

Throughout my K-12 education, school and I didn't get along. I graduated near the bottom of my small high school class and had no plans on going to college. Yet, dragged kicking and screaming, I earned an Associate degree from community college in northern Illinois, while earning a black belt in Kung-fu. I fully intended on opening my own martial arts studio, *not* continuing on in college. Learning subjects seemed far less important than learning about life.

Then I found my passion in the field of philosophy. Luckily, I had the right people in my life to encourage me to pursue my dreams in the face of those who couldn't stop asking, "What are you going to do with a philosophy degree?" My canned response to that question was always, "Actually, I am going to take over the world."

I earned a Bachelor's Degree in the Honors Program at Montana State University with a dual major in Philosophy of Religion and Psychology, then a Master's degree in Philosophy of Religion and Ethics from Biola University.

After a few brief years in the corporate world, my desire to coach and teach led me to take a position at a large church in Salem, Oregon. There, I launched a large public speaking/seminar ministry called the Apollos Forum that drew audiences of 400 – 500 people regularly.

I almost became another college dropout statistic. Instead I earned Master's degree and landed a job doing what I love against all odds. The work I focus most on today is helping students like me find their way, get motivated, and bring out their passion. In addition to writing and teaching - both in the classroom and online, I now teach 1 - 3 day writing seminars to incoming college students around the country to help them achieve similar results.

For more information on Scott Matkovich, visit:
www.youversustheworld.com

ASIN: B0054EXBH6

Made in the USA
Lexington, KY
29 June 2014